Axton Nexus

# C++
## Programming for GUI Development With wxWidgets and Qt

A Hands-On Beginner's Guide to Using wxWidgets and Qt for Building Fast, Reliable, and User-Friendly Desktop Applications

# Table Of content

# Disclaimer

The information provided in this book, "C++ Programming for GUI Development with wxWidgets and Qt," is intended for educational and informational purposes only. While every effort has been made to ensure the accuracy and completeness of[1] the content, the author and publisher make no representations or warranties of any kind, express or implied, about the completeness, accuracy, reliability,[2] suitability, or availability with respect to the book or the information, products, services, or related graphics contained in the book for any purpose. Any reliance you place on such information is therefore strictly at your own risk.[3]

The code examples and projects in this book are provided as illustrations and learning tools. They may not be suitable for production environments without further adaptation and testing. The author and publisher shall not be liable for any errors, omissions, or damages arising from the use of the code or projects.

This book may contain links to third-party websites or resources. These links are provided for convenience and informational purposes only.[4] The author and publisher have no control over the content of these external websites and do not endorse or guarantee their accuracy, relevance, or availability.

The technologies and frameworks covered in this book (wxWidgets and Qt) are subject to change and updates. The author and publisher make no warranty that the information provided in this book will remain current or accurate over time. It is recommended to refer to the official documentation and resources for the latest information on wxWidgets and Qt.

The views and opinions expressed in this book are solely those of the author and do not necessarily reflect the views of the publisher.[5]

This book is not intended to provide legal, financial, or professional advice. If you require specific advice, please consult with a qualified professional.

The author and publisher shall not be liable for any loss or damage including without limitation, indirect or consequential loss or damage, or any loss or damage whatsoever arising from loss of data or profits arising out of, or in connection with, the use of this[6] book.

By using this book, you agree to the terms of this disclaimer.

**Copyright Notice**

This book is protected by copyright. No part of this book may be reproduced, distributed, or transmitted in any form or by any means, including photocopying,[7] recording, or other electronic or mechanical methods, without the prior written permission of the publisher, except in the case of brief quotations embodied in critical reviews and certain other[8] noncommercial uses permitted by copyright law.

## Trademarks

All trademarks,[9] service marks, and trade names used in this book are the property of their respective owners.

# Introduction

Welcome to the world of C++ GUI development! This book, **"C++ Programming for GUI Development with wxWidgets and Qt: A Hands-On Guide to Building Fast, Reliable, and User-Friendly Desktop Applications,"** is your comprehensive guide to mastering the art of crafting visually appealing, responsive, and efficient graphical user interfaces using two of the most powerful C++ frameworks: wxWidgets and Qt.

In today's technology-driven world, user experience is paramount. Whether you're developing applications for business, entertainment, education, or scientific research, a well-designed graphical interface is crucial for engaging users and ensuring your software stands out from the crowd. C++, with its performance and versatility, remains a top choice for building high-quality desktop applications, and wxWidgets and Qt provide the ideal frameworks for bringing your GUI visions to life.

This book is designed for both aspiring and experienced C++ developers who want to delve into the world of GUI programming. We'll take a hands-on approach, guiding you through the fundamental concepts and techniques, while building practical projects and exploring real-world examples. From basic controls and layouts to advanced topics like custom widget creation, multithreading, and cross-platform considerations, you'll gain the knowledge and skills needed to create professional-grade GUI applications that are not only visually appealing but also robust, efficient, and user-friendly.

**What sets this book apart:**

- **Comprehensive Coverage:** We explore both wxWidgets and Qt, giving you a broad perspective and the freedom to choose the framework that best suits your needs.
- **Hands-On Approach:** Learn by doing with practical examples, coding exercises, and project guidelines that reinforce your understanding.
- **Real-World Focus:** Gain insights into building real-world applications, including a text editor, a data visualization tool, and a networked game.
- **Cross-Platform Emphasis:** Learn how to create applications that work seamlessly on Windows, macOS, and Linux.
- **Best Practices and Common Mistakes:** We highlight best practices and common pitfalls to help you write clean, efficient, and maintainable code.

**By the end of this book, you'll be able to:**

- Confidently use wxWidgets and Qt to build cross-platform GUI applications.
- Design user interfaces with a variety of controls, layouts, and visual elements.
- Handle user input, events, and multithreading for responsive and interactive applications.
- Implement advanced features like custom widgets, graphics, and networking.
- Package and deploy your applications for different operating systems.

So, embark on this exciting journey into the world of C++ GUI development! With dedication and this book as your guide, you'll be well on your way to creating impressive and user-friendly desktop applications that make a real impact.

# Part I: Foundations

# Chapter 1: Introduction to GUI Programming

## What is a GUI?

In the early days of computing, interacting with a computer was a daunting task. Users had to memorize complex commands and type them into a cryptic interface known as the command-line interface (CLI). Imagine having to remember and type mkdir myfolder just to create a simple folder! Fortunately, the world of computing underwent a revolution with the advent of the **Graphical User Interface (GUI)**.

A GUI provides a visual way to interact with a computer using elements like **windows, icons, menus, and pointers**. Instead of typing obscure commands, you can simply click a button, drag an icon, or select an option from a menu. This visual approach makes computers much more intuitive and user-friendly, opening up the digital world to a wider audience.

Think about your everyday interactions with your computer or smartphone. Every time you open an application, browse the web, or play a game, you are interacting with a GUI. The icons on your desktop, the buttons in your web browser, the menus in your word processor – these are all elements of a GUI.

**Key characteristics of a GUI:**

- **Visual Representation:** GUIs use visual elements to represent objects and actions, making them easier to understand and remember.
- **Intuitive Interaction:** GUIs allow users to interact with the computer in a natural and intuitive way, using actions like clicking, dragging, and dropping.
- **WYSIWYG (What You See Is What You Get):** GUIs provide a visual representation of the final output, allowing users to see the results of their actions immediately.
- **Flexibility:** GUIs can be customized to suit different user preferences and needs.

**Benefits of using a GUI:**

- **Ease of Use:** GUIs are much easier to learn and use than CLIs, making them accessible to a wider range of users.
- **Increased Efficiency:** GUIs allow users to perform tasks more quickly and efficiently by providing direct manipulation of objects and actions.
- **Improved User Experience:** GUIs provide a more engaging and enjoyable user experience, making computers more appealing to use.
- **Enhanced Productivity:** GUIs can help users to be more productive by providing a streamlined

workflow and reducing the need for memorization.

**Examples of GUIs:**

- **Desktop operating systems:** Windows, macOS, Linux
- **Web browsers:** Chrome, Firefox, Safari
- **Mobile operating systems:** Android, iOS
- **Applications:** Microsoft Office, Adobe Photoshop, Games

**The evolution of GUIs:**

GUIs have come a long way since their early days. They have evolved from simple, monochrome interfaces to sophisticated, high-resolution displays with rich visuals and animations. This evolution has been driven by advances in technology, such as increased processing power, better graphics capabilities, and new input devices like touchscreens.

**The future of GUIs:**

As technology continues to advance, we can expect GUIs to become even more sophisticated and immersive. We may see the emergence of new interaction paradigms, such as voice control, gesture recognition, and augmented reality. The goal remains the same: to make interacting with computers as natural and intuitive as possible.

In the context of this book, we will be focusing on building GUIs for desktop applications using C++ and two powerful frameworks: wxWidgets and Qt. These frameworks provide a rich set of tools and libraries for creating cross-platform GUIs that are fast, reliable, and user-friendly.

## Why C++ for GUI Development?

While many programming languages and frameworks exist for building GUIs, C++ holds a special place, particularly when crafting high-performance, robust, and versatile desktop applications. Here's why:

### 1. Performance and Efficiency:

- **Raw Power:** C++ is renowned for its performance. It allows direct memory manipulation and fine-grained control over system hardware, enabling the creation of highly optimized applications that respond quickly and efficiently to user interactions. This is crucial for GUI applications where smooth animations, rapid rendering, and minimal lag are essential for a positive user experience.

- **Resource Management:** C++ gives developers explicit control over memory management. While this comes with responsibility, it also allows for the creation of applications with minimal overhead and efficient resource utilization, critical for resource-intensive GUI programs.

## 2. Cross-Platform Compatibility:

- **Write Once, Run Anywhere:** C++ code can be compiled on various platforms (Windows, macOS, Linux) with minimal changes. This portability is invaluable for GUI development, allowing you to reach a wider audience with a single codebase.
- **Established Frameworks:** wxWidgets and Qt, the focus of this book, are powerful cross-platform GUI frameworks designed for C++. They provide a consistent API and handle platform-specific nuances, making it easier to develop applications that look and feel native on different operating systems.

## 3. Flexibility and Control:

- **Low-Level Access:** C++ provides low-level access to system APIs and hardware, giving developers the flexibility to integrate with specialized devices or implement custom functionalities within their GUI applications.

- **Paradigm Choice:** C++ supports both procedural and object-oriented programming (OOP) paradigms. This allows you to choose the approach that best suits your project's needs and complexity.

### 4. Extensive Libraries and Tools:

- **Rich Ecosystem:** C++ boasts a vast ecosystem of libraries and tools for GUI development. This includes everything from graphics rendering libraries (like OpenGL) to networking libraries for building connected applications.
- **Community Support:** A large and active C++ community provides ample resources, forums, and documentation to assist developers at all levels.

### 5. Industry Standards:

- **Wide Adoption:** C++ remains a popular choice for developing high-performance applications in various industries, including game development, finance, and scientific computing. Many existing GUI applications are built with C++, ensuring its relevance and longevity.
- **Legacy Code:** A significant amount of legacy code is written in C++. Knowing C++ allows you

to maintain and extend these applications, many of which have GUI components.

**C++ in the Modern GUI Landscape**

While languages like Python and JavaScript have gained popularity for GUI development due to their ease of use and rapid prototyping capabilities, C++ continues to be favored when performance, efficiency, and control are paramount. It remains the go-to language for building complex, resource-intensive GUI applications that demand a high level of responsiveness and customization.

By learning C++ and mastering frameworks like wxWidgets and Qt, you'll be equipped to build robust, cross-platform GUI applications that meet the demands of today's users and stand the test of time.

## wxWidgets vs. Qt: A Comparison

Both wxWidgets and Qt are leading cross-platform GUI frameworks for C++, offering a rich set of tools and libraries for building high-quality desktop applications. While they share the goal of simplifying GUI development, they differ in their philosophies, licensing models, and features. This section provides a comparative overview to help you understand their strengths and weaknesses.

**wxWidgets**

- **Philosophy:** wxWidgets aims to provide a native look and feel on each platform by using the platform's native widgets whenever possible.[1] This results in applications that blend seamlessly with the user's operating system.
- **Licensing:** wxWidgets is licensed under the wxWindows Library Licence, a permissive open-source license similar to the LGPL.[2] This allows you to use wxWidgets in both open-source and commercial projects with minimal restrictions.[3]
- **Features:**
  - **Native Look and Feel:** wxWidgets applications tend to look and feel like native applications on each platform.
  - **Small Footprint:** wxWidgets is known for its relatively small size, resulting in smaller executables.
  - **Active Community:** wxWidgets has a dedicated and active community that provides support and contributes to its development.[4]

**Qt**

- **Philosophy:** Qt offers a comprehensive framework for GUI development, providing its own set of widgets and tools that render consistently across platforms.[5] This ensures a uniform look and feel regardless of the operating system.

- **Licensing:** Qt offers both commercial and open-source licenses.[6] The open-source version is licensed under the GPL and LGPL, while the commercial license provides more flexibility for proprietary applications.[7]
- **Features:**
  - **Comprehensive Framework:** Qt provides a wider range of features beyond GUI development, including networking, database connectivity, and multimedia support.[8]
  - **Qt Designer:** Qt includes a powerful visual design tool called Qt Designer, which allows you to create user interfaces by dragging and dropping widgets.[9]
  - **QML:** Qt offers QML, a declarative language for creating modern and fluid user interfaces.[10]

## Comparison Table

| Feature | wxWidgets | Qt |
|---------|-----------|-----|

| | | |
|---|---|---|
| **Look and Feel** | Native | Consistent across platforms |
| **Licensing** | Permissive open-source (wxWindows Library Licence) | Commercial and open-source (GPL/LGPL) |
| **Size** | Smaller footprint | Larger footprint |
| **Design Tool** | No dedicated design tool | Qt Designer |
| **QML Support** | No | Yes |
| **Extra Features** | Fewer extra features | More comprehensive framework (networking, database, multimedia) |
| **Learning Curve** | Relatively easier for beginners | Steeper learning curve due to its wider scope |
| **Community** | Active and dedicated | Large and well-established |

**Choosing the Right Framework**

The choice between wxWidgets and Qt depends on your specific needs and priorities.

- **Choose wxWidgets if:**
  - You prioritize a native look and feel.
  - You need a smaller footprint for your application.
  - You prefer a permissive open-source license.
- **Choose Qt if:**
  - You need a consistent look and feel across platforms.
  - You require a comprehensive framework with extra features.
  - You want to use a visual design tool like Qt Designer.
  - You are interested in using QML for modern UI design.

Ultimately, the best way to decide is to experiment with both frameworks and see which one best suits your development style and project requirements. This book will provide you with the knowledge and skills to work with both wxWidgets and Qt, empowering you to make an informed decision and build high-quality GUI applications with confidence.

# Setting Up Your Development Environment (Windows, macOS, Linux)

Before diving into the exciting world of GUI programming with C++, wxWidgets, and Qt, you need to set up your development environment. This involves installing the necessary tools and configuring your system to compile and run C++ code. This section provides a step-by-step guide for Windows, macOS, and Linux.

## 1. Choose an IDE (Integrated Development Environment)

An IDE provides a comprehensive environment for writing, compiling, debugging, and running your code. Popular choices for C++ development include:

- **Code::Blocks:** A free, open-source, cross-platform IDE. (Recommended for beginners)
- **Visual Studio:** A powerful IDE from Microsoft, primarily for Windows development. (Excellent debugger and Windows-specific features)
- **Qt Creator:** The official IDE for Qt development, available on all platforms. (Great for Qt projects, but can be used for general C++ as well)

- **CLion:** A cross-platform IDE from JetBrains with advanced features and excellent code analysis. (Commercial license, but offers a free trial)

## 2. Install a C++ Compiler

A compiler translates your C++ code into machine-readable instructions.

- **Windows:** Visual Studio comes with a built-in compiler. You can also install MinGW, a popular open-source compiler suite.
- **macOS:** Xcode, available from the Mac App Store, includes a C++ compiler.
- **Linux:** Most Linux distributions come with GCC (GNU Compiler Collection) pre-installed. You can install it using your distribution's package manager if it's not already available.

## 3. Install wxWidgets

- **Windows:**
  - Download the wxWidgets installer from the official website (wxwidgets.org).
  - Run the installer and follow the on-screen instructions.
  - Choose a build configuration (e.g., "Release" or "Debug") and the desired

GUI toolkit (e.g., "wxMSW" for native Windows look).

- **macOS:**
  - Use Homebrew: brew install wxwidgets
  - Or download the source code and build it manually.
- **Linux:**
  - Use your distribution's package manager (e.g., sudo apt-get install libwxgtk3.0-dev on Debian/Ubuntu).
  - Or download the source code and build it manually.

### 4. Install Qt

- **Windows:**
  - Download the Qt online installer from the official website (qt.io).
  - Run the installer and select the desired components (Qt Creator, Qt libraries, compilers).
- **macOS:**
  - Use Homebrew: brew install qt
  - Or download the online installer.
- **Linux:**
  - Use your distribution's package manager (e.g., sudo apt-get install qt5-default on Debian/Ubuntu).
  - Or download the online installer.

## 5. Configure your IDE

- **Code::Blocks:**
    - Create a new project and select "wxWidgets project."
    - Follow the wizard to configure the project settings, including the wxWidgets installation directory.
- **Visual Studio:**
    - Create a new project and select "Empty Project."
    - Configure the project properties to include the wxWidgets header files and libraries.
- **Qt Creator:**
    - Create a new project and select "Qt Widgets Application."
    - Qt Creator automatically configures the project for Qt development.

## 6. Test Your Setup

- **wxWidgets:**
    - Create a simple "Hello, World!" program using wxWidgets.
    - Compile and run the program to ensure that wxWidgets is correctly installed and configured.
- **Qt:**

- Create a simple "Hello, World!" program using Qt.
- Compile and run the program using Qt Creator.

**Example "Hello, World!" program (wxWidgets):**

C++

```cpp
#include <wx/wxprec.h>
#ifndef WX_PRECOMP
    #include <wx/wx.h>
#endif


class MyApp : public wxApp
{
public:
    virtual bool OnInit();
};


class MyFrame : public wxFrame
{
```

```cpp
public:
    MyFrame(const wxString& title, const wxPoint& pos,
const wxSize& size);
private:
    void OnHello(wxCommandEvent& event);

    void OnExit(wxCommandEvent& event);

    void OnAbout(wxCommandEvent& event);

    wxDECLARE_EVENT_TABLE();
};


enum
{
    ID_Hello = 1
};


wxBEGIN_EVENT_TABLE(MyFrame, wxFrame)
    EVT_MENU(ID_Hello,   MyFrame::OnHello)
    EVT_MENU(wxID_EXIT, MyFrame::OnExit)
```

```cpp
    EVT_MENU(wxID_ABOUT, MyFrame::OnAbout)
wxEND_EVENT_TABLE()


wxIMPLEMENT_APP(MyApp);


bool MyApp::OnInit()
{
    MyFrame *frame = new MyFrame( "Hello World",
wxPoint(50, 50), wxSize(450, 340) );
    frame->Show( true );
    return true;
}


MyFrame::MyFrame(const    wxString&    title,    const
wxPoint& pos, const wxSize& size)
        : wxFrame(NULL, wxID_ANY, title, pos, size)
{
    wxMenu *menuFile = new wxMenu;
    menuFile->Append(ID_Hello, "&Hello...\tCtrl-H",
```

```cpp
                        "Help string shown in status bar for this
menu item");

    menuFile->AppendSeparator();

    menuFile->Append(wxID_EXIT);

    wxMenu *menuHelp = new wxMenu;

    menuHelp->Append(wxID_ABOUT);

    wxMenuBar *menuBar = new wxMenuBar;

    menuBar->Append( menuFile, "&File" );

    menuBar->Append( menuHelp, "&Help" );

    SetMenuBar( menuBar );

    CreateStatusBar();

    SetStatusText( "Welcome to wxWidgets!" );
}


void MyFrame::OnExit(wxCommandEvent& event)
{
    Close( true );
}
```

```cpp
void MyFrame::OnAbout(wxCommandEvent& event)

{

    wxMessageBox( "This is a wxWidgets' Hello world sample",

                        "About Hello World", wxOK | wxICON_INFORMATION );

}


void MyFrame::OnHello(wxCommandEvent& event)

{

    wxLogMessage("Hello world from wxWidgets!");

}
```

This setup process provides a solid foundation for your C++ GUI development journey. With your IDE and frameworks in place, you're ready to start building your first GUI applications. Remember to consult the official documentation for wxWidgets and Qt for detailed installation instructions and troubleshooting tips specific to your operating system and chosen IDE.

# Practice: Setting up your preferred IDE (e.g., Code::Blocks, Visual Studio, Qt Creator)

Now that you have a general understanding of the setup process, let's get hands-on and configure your preferred IDE for C++ GUI development. This section provides specific instructions and practice exercises for three popular IDEs: Code::Blocks, Visual Studio, and Qt Creator.

## Code::Blocks

1. **Installation:**
   - Download the Code::Blocks installer with the MinGW compiler from the official website (codeblocks.org).
   - Run the installer and follow the on-screen instructions.
2. **Creating a wxWidgets Project:**
   - Open Code::Blocks and go to **File > New > Project...**
   - Select **wxWidgets project** and click **Go**.
   - Follow the wizard, providing the project name, location, and wxWidgets installation directory.
   - Choose the appropriate GUI toolkit (e.g., wxMSW for Windows).
   - Click **Finish** to create the project.
3. **Building and Running:**

- Code::Blocks will generate a basic wxWidgets "Hello, World!" application.
- Build the project by clicking the **Build** icon or pressing **Ctrl+F9**.
- Run the project by clicking the **Run** icon or pressing **F9**.
- You should see a window with a menu bar and a status bar.

**Practice:**

- Modify the generated code to add a button to the window.
- Connect the button to an event handler that displays a message box when clicked.
- Experiment with different wxWidgets controls (e.g., text boxes, checkboxes) and add them to your application.

**Visual Studio**

1. **Installation:**
   - Download Visual Studio Community edition from the official website (visualstudio.microsoft.com).
   - Run the installer and select the "Desktop development with C++" workload.
2. **Creating a wxWidgets Project:**
   - Open Visual Studio and go to **File > New > Project...**

- Select **Empty Project** and click **Create**.
- Right-click on the project in the Solution Explorer and go to **Properties**.
- In the **VC++ Directories** section, add the include and library directories of your wxWidgets installation.
- In the **Linker > Input** section, add the necessary wxWidgets libraries (e.g., wxmsw31ud.lib).
- Create a new source file (.cpp) and add the wxWidgets "Hello, World!" code from the previous section.

3. **Building and Running:**
   - Build the project by clicking the **Build** icon or pressing **Ctrl+Shift+B**.
   - Run the project by clicking the **Start** icon or pressing **F5**.
   - You should see a window with a menu bar and a status bar.

**Practice:**

- Explore the different project settings in Visual Studio.
- Use the debugger to step through the code and understand how the application works.
- Create a new project and try using Qt instead of wxWidgets. Configure the project properties accordingly.

**Qt Creator**

1. **Installation:**
   - Download the Qt online installer from the official website (qt.io).
   - Run the installer and select Qt Creator, the desired Qt libraries, and a compiler.

2. **Creating a Qt Project:**
   - Open Qt Creator and go to **File > New File or Project...**
   - Select **Qt Widgets Application** and click **Choose**.
   - Follow the wizard, providing the project name and location.
   - Choose the appropriate kit (compiler and Qt version).
   - Click **Finish** to create the project.

3. **Building and Running:**
   - Qt Creator will generate a basic Qt "Hello, World!" application.
   - Build the project by clicking the **Build** icon or pressing **Ctrl+B**.
   - Run the project by clicking the **Run** icon or pressing **Ctrl+R**.
   - You should see a window with a title bar and a central widget.

**Practice:**

- Use Qt Designer to design the user interface of your application.
- Explore the Qt documentation and learn about different Qt widgets and layouts.
- Create a new project and try using QML to design a modern user interface.

By completing these practice exercises, you'll gain valuable experience in setting up your preferred IDE for C++ GUI development. This will lay a solid foundation for the rest of the book, where you'll learn to build more complex and sophisticated GUI applications using wxWidgets and Qt.

# Chapter 2: C++ Essentials for GUI Development

## Core Language Features: Variables, Data Types, Operators, Control Flow

This chapter provides a foundation in the core C++ language features essential for GUI programming. While we won't cover every aspect of C++, we'll focus on the building blocks you'll use most frequently when creating GUI applications with wxWidgets and Qt.

**Core Language Features**

**1. Variables**

Variables are like containers that hold data in your program. They have a name and a data type that determines what kind of information they can store.

- **Declaration:** data_type variable_name; (e.g., int age;, double price;, std::string name;)
- **Assignment:** variable_name = value; (e.g., age = 25;, price = 9.99;, name = "John Doe";)
- **Initialization:** data_type variable_name = value; (e.g., int age = 25;)

**Common Data Types:**

- **int:** Stores whole numbers (e.g., 10, -5, 0).
- **double:** Stores floating-point numbers (e.g., 3.14, -2.5).
- **char:** Stores single characters (e.g., 'A', '$', '?').
- **bool:** Stores boolean values (true or false).
- **std::string:** Stores sequences of characters (e.g., "Hello, world!").

## 2. Operators

Operators perform operations on data.

- **Arithmetic Operators:** +, -, *, /, % (modulo)
- **Comparison Operators:** == (equals), != (not equals), >, <, >=, <=
- **Logical Operators:** && (and), || (or), ! (not)
- **Assignment Operators:** =, +=, -=, *=, /=, %=

## 3. Control Flow

Control flow statements determine the order in which your code is executed.

- **Conditional Statements:**
  - **if:** Executes a block of code if a condition is true.
  - **else if:** Executes a block of code if a previous condition is false and another condition is true.

- **else:** Executes a block of code if all previous conditions are false.

C++

```
if (age >= 18) {
    // Code to execute if age is 18 or older
} else {
    // Code to execute if age is less than 18
}
```

- **Loops:**
  - **for:** Repeats a block of code a specific number of times.

C++

```
for (int i = 0; i < 10; i++) {
    // Code to execute 10 times
}
```

- **while:** Repeats a block of code as long as a condition is true.

C++

```
while (x > 0) {
    // Code to execute while x is greater than 0
}
```

- **do-while:** Similar to while, but the code block is executed at least once.

C++

```
do {
    // Code to execute at least once
} while (x > 0);
```

- **Switch Statement:** Selects one of many code blocks to execute based on the value of an expression.

C++

```cpp
switch (dayOfWeek) {
    case 1:
        // Code for Monday
        break;
    case 2:
        // Code for Tuesday
        break;
    // ...
    default:
        // Code for other days
        break;
}
```

## 4. Functions

Functions are reusable blocks of code that perform specific tasks.

- **Definition:**

C++

```
return_type function_name(parameter_list) {

    // Code to execute

    return value; // (if the function returns a value)

}
```

- **Calling:** function_name(arguments);

**Example:**

C++

```cpp
int calculateArea(int width, int height) {

    int area = width * height;

    return area;

}


int main() {

    int result = calculateArea(5, 10); // result will be 50

    return 0;

}
```

These core language features form the foundation for writing any C++ program, including GUI applications. Understanding them thoroughly will enable you to write clean, efficient, and maintainable code. In the following sections, we'll explore more advanced C++ concepts that are particularly relevant to GUI development.

## Object-Oriented Programming (OOP) in C++: Classes, Objects, Inheritance, Polymorphism

Object-oriented programming (OOP) is a powerful paradigm that allows you to structure your code around "objects" – self-contained units that combine data and the operations that act on that data. This approach brings modularity, reusability, and flexibility to your programs, making it particularly well-suited for GUI development where you often deal with many interactive elements.

## 1. Classes

Classes are blueprints for creating objects. They define the structure and behavior of objects by specifying:

- **Data members:** Variables that hold the object's data (attributes).
- **Member functions:** Functions that operate on the object's data (methods).

**Example:**

```cpp
C++

class Button {
public:
    std::string label;
    int positionX;
    int positionY;
```

```cpp
void onClick() {

    // Code to execute when the button is clicked

}
};
```

## 2. Objects

Objects are instances of classes. They have their own unique set of data members, but they share the same member functions defined by their class.

**Example:**

C++

```cpp
Button myButton;

myButton.label = "Click Me";

myButton.positionX = 100;

myButton.positionY = 50;

myButton.onClick(); // Call the onClick function of myButton
```

## 3. Inheritance

Inheritance allows you to create new classes (derived classes) based on existing classes (base classes). The derived[1] class inherits the data members and member functions of the base class, and can add its own unique features.

**Example:**

C++

```
class ImageButton : public Button {
public:
    std::string imagePath;


    void displayImage() {
        // Code to display the image
    }
};
```

In this example, ImageButton inherits from Button, so it has all the features of a Button (label, position, onClick()

function) plus an additional imagePath and a displayImage() function.

## 4. Polymorphism

Polymorphism allows objects of different classes to be treated as objects of a common type. This is achieved through:

- **Virtual Functions:** Base class functions that can be overridden in derived classes to provide specific behavior.

**Example:**

C++

```cpp
class Shape {
public:
  virtual void draw() {
    // Default drawing behavior
  }
};


class Circle : public Shape {
```

```cpp
public:
    void draw() override {
        // Code to draw a circle
    }
};


class Rectangle : public Shape {
public:
    void draw() override {
        // Code to draw a rectangle
    }
};
```

With polymorphism, you can treat Circle and Rectangle objects as Shape objects, and call their draw() function. The correct version of draw() (specific to the object's actual class) will be executed at runtime.

**Benefits of OOP in GUI Development:**

- **Modularity:** GUI components (buttons, windows, menus) can be represented as objects, making the code more organized and easier to understand.
- **Reusability:** Inheritance allows you to create new GUI components by extending existing ones, reducing code duplication.
- **Flexibility:** Polymorphism enables you to treat different GUI components in a uniform way, simplifying event handling and UI logic.
- **Maintainability:** OOP principles promote code that is easier to maintain, modify, and extend over time.

By understanding and applying OOP concepts, you can write more robust, efficient, and scalable GUI applications in C++. This foundation will be crucial as you delve into the wxWidgets and Qt frameworks, which heavily rely on OOP principles.

## Memory Management: Pointers, Dynamic Allocation, and Avoiding Memory Leaks

Memory management is a critical aspect of C++ programming, especially when building GUI applications that often handle complex data structures and user interactions. Understanding how to manage memory effectively is crucial for writing efficient, stable, and reliable programs.

## 1. Pointers

Pointers are variables that store memory addresses. They allow you to directly access and manipulate data stored in memory.

- **Declaration:** data_type *pointer_name; (e.g., int *ptr;, char *strPtr;)
- **Address-of operator (&):** Obtains the memory address of a variable (e.g., ptr = &myVariable;).
- **Dereference operator (*):** Accesses the value stored at the memory address pointed to by a pointer (e.g., int value = *ptr;).

## 2. Dynamic Memory Allocation

Dynamic memory allocation allows you to allocate memory during program execution, providing flexibility for handling data structures that vary in size.

- new **operator:** Allocates memory for a single object or an array of objects.
  - pointer_name = new data_type; (e.g., int *ptr = new int;)
  - pointer_name = new data_type[size]; (e.g., int *arr = new int[10];)

- delete **operator:** Releases memory allocated with new.
  - delete pointer_name; (for single objects)
  - delete[] pointer_name; (for arrays)

## 3. Memory Leaks

A memory leak occurs when you allocate memory dynamically but fail to release it when it's no longer needed. This can lead to your program consuming more and more memory over time, eventually causing performance degradation or even crashes.

**Common Causes of Memory Leaks:**

- **Forgetting to** delete **allocated memory.**
- **Losing track of pointers to allocated memory.**
- **Exceptions or errors that prevent** delete **from being called.**

## 4. Avoiding Memory Leaks

- **Always** delete **what you** new**:** Make sure to release dynamically allocated memory when you're finished with it.
- **Use RAII (Resource Acquisition Is Initialization):** This technique encapsulates resource management (like memory) within objects, ensuring that resources are automatically released when the object goes out of scope.

- **Smart Pointers:** C++ provides smart pointers (std::unique_ptr, std::shared_ptr) that automatically manage memory for you.

C++

**#include** <memory>

```
std::unique_ptr<int> ptr(new int); // ptr automatically deletes the int when it goes out of scope
```

```
std::shared_ptr<int> sharedPtr1(new int);
std::shared_ptr<int> sharedPtr2 = sharedPtr1; // Both pointers share ownership of the int
```

- **Valgrind:** This tool can help you detect memory leaks in your programs.

**Best Practices**

- **Minimize dynamic allocation:** If possible, use stack-allocated variables instead of dynamic allocation.
- **Handle exceptions carefully:** Ensure that delete is called even if an exception occurs.
- **Write clean and organized code:** This makes it easier to track memory allocation and deallocation.

By understanding pointers, dynamic allocation, and the causes of memory leaks, you can write C++ GUI applications that are both efficient and reliable. Employing smart pointers and following best practices will help you avoid memory-related issues and ensure the long-term stability of your programs.

## Common Mistakes: Dangling pointers, memory leaks

While pointers and dynamic memory allocation are powerful tools in C++, they can also lead to subtle and frustrating errors if not handled carefully. Two of the most common pitfalls are dangling pointers and memory leaks.

### 1. Dangling Pointers

A dangling pointer is a pointer that points to a memory location that has been deallocated or is no longer valid.

Accessing a dangling pointer can lead to unpredictable[1] behavior, crashes, or data corruption.

**Causes of Dangling Pointers:**

- **Deleting memory that is still being pointed to:**

C++

```
int *ptr = new int;

delete ptr;

*ptr = 10; // Error: ptr is now a dangling pointer
```

- **Returning a pointer to a local variable:**

C++

```
int* createInt() {

    int x = 5;

    return &x; // Error: x goes out of scope when the function returns
```

}

- **Multiple pointers pointing to the same memory, and one of them deallocates it:**

C++

int *ptr1 = new int;

int *ptr2 = ptr1;

delete ptr1;

*ptr2 = 10; // Error: ptr2 is now a dangling pointer

## 2. Memory Leaks

A memory leak occurs when you allocate memory dynamically using new but fail to deallocate it using delete when it's no longer needed. This can lead to your program gradually consuming more and more memory, potentially causing performance issues or even crashes.

**Causes of Memory Leaks:**

- **Forgetting to delete:**

C++

```
int *ptr = new int;

// ... code that uses ptr ...

// Error: ptr is never deleted, causing a memory leak
```

- **Losing track of pointers:**

C++

```
void myFunction() {

    int *ptr = new int;

    // ... code that uses ptr ...
```

// Error: ptr goes out of scope, and the allocated memory is lost

```
}
```

- **Exceptions:**

C++

```
try {
    int *ptr = new int;
    // ... code that might throw an exception ...
    delete ptr;
} catch (...) {
```
// Error: If an exception is thrown, delete ptr is not executed

```
}
```

### How to Avoid These Mistakes

- **Be mindful of memory ownership:** Keep track of which part of your code is responsible for deallocating memory.
- **Use smart pointers:** Smart pointers (std::unique_ptr, std::shared_ptr) automatically manage memory for you, reducing the risk of leaks and dangling pointers.
- **Follow RAII (Resource Acquisition Is Initialization):** Encapsulate resource management within objects to ensure proper allocation and deallocation.
- **Write clean and organized code:** This makes it easier to track memory usage and avoid errors.
- **Use tools like Valgrind:** Valgrind can help you detect memory leaks and other memory-related errors in your code.

By being aware of these common mistakes and following best practices, you can write C++ GUI applications that are robust, efficient, and free from memory-related problems.

# Best Practices: RAII (Resource Acquisition Is Initialization), smart pointers

As we've seen, manual memory management in C++ can be error-prone. Fortunately, C++ offers powerful tools and idioms to help you manage memory safely and efficiently. Two of the most important are RAII and smart pointers.

## 1. RAII (Resource Acquisition Is Initialization)

RAII is a programming idiom that ties resource management (such as memory allocation) to the lifespan of objects. The core idea is to acquire a resource in the constructor of an object and release it in the destructor. This ensures that the resource is automatically released when the object goes out of scope, even if exceptions occur.

**Example:**

```cpp
C++

#include <iostream>


class FileHandler {
```

```cpp
public:

    FileHandler(const std::string& filename) :
file(filename) {

    if (!file.is_open()) {

    throw std::runtime_error("Failed to open file");

    }

        std::cout << "File opened successfully." <<
std::endl;

    }


    ~FileHandler() {

    if (file.is_open()) {

    file.close();

    std::cout << "File closed." << std::endl;

    }

    }
```

```cpp
private:

    std::fstream file;

};


int main() {

    try {

        FileHandler fh("my_file.txt");

        // ... code that uses the file ...

    } catch (const std::runtime_error& error) {

        std::cerr << "Error: " << error.what() << std::endl;

    }

    // File is automatically closed when fh goes out of
scope

    return 0;

}
```

In this example, the FileHandler class acquires the file resource in its constructor and releases it in its destructor. Even if an exception is thrown while using the file, the destructor will be called, ensuring that the file is closed properly.

## 2. Smart Pointers

Smart pointers are classes that wrap raw pointers and provide automatic memory management. They automatically deallocate the memory they point to when they go out of scope or when their ownership is transferred.

C++ offers several types of smart pointers:

- std::unique_ptr: Represents exclusive ownership of a resource. Only one unique_ptr can point to a given object at a time. When the unique_ptr goes out of scope, the object is automatically deleted.

C++

```
#include <memory>


std::unique_ptr<int> ptr(new int);

// ... use ptr ...
```

// Memory is automatically deleted when ptr goes out of scope

- std::shared_ptr: Allows multiple shared_ptrs to share ownership of a resource. The object is deleted when the last shared_ptr pointing to it goes out of scope.

C++

```
#include <memory>
```

```
std::shared_ptr<int> ptr1(new int);

std::shared_ptr<int> ptr2 = ptr1; // Both ptr1 and ptr2 own the int

// ... use ptr1 and ptr2 ...

// Memory is deleted when both ptr1 and ptr2 go out of scope
```

- std::weak_ptr: Provides a non-owning "weak" reference to an object managed by a shared_ptr. It can be used to break circular dependencies and prevent memory leaks.

**Benefits of Using RAII and Smart Pointers:**

- **Reduced risk of memory leaks:** Automatic resource management prevents memory leaks.
- **Improved code clarity:** Code becomes cleaner and easier to read as resource management is handled automatically.
- **Exception safety:** Resources are released even if exceptions occur.
- **Simplified resource sharing:** shared_ptr allows safe sharing of resources between different parts of your code.

By adopting RAII and using smart pointers, you can significantly improve the safety and reliability of your C++ GUI applications, freeing you to focus on the core logic of your program.

## Code samples: Demonstrating proper memory management techniques

C++

```cpp
#include <iostream>

#include <memory>



// Example 1: Using RAII for managing a
dynamically allocated array

class DynamicArray {

public:

          DynamicArray(size_t   size)   :
size_(size), data_(new int[size]) {

        std::cout << "Array of size " <<
size_ << " created." << std::endl;

    }



    ~DynamicArray() {

        delete[] data_;

        std::cout << "Array deleted." <<
std::endl;

    }
```

```cpp
    // ... other member functions to access
and manipulate the array ...


private:

    size_t size_;

    int* data_;

};



// Example 2: Using unique_ptr to manage a
dynamically allocated object

class Widget {

public:

        Widget() { std::cout << "Widget
created." << std::endl; }

        ~Widget() { std::cout << "Widget
deleted." << std::endl; }

    // ... other member functions ...

};
```

```cpp
// Example 3: Using shared_ptr for shared
ownership

void   processWidget(std::shared_ptr<Widget>
w) {

    // ... use the widget ...

}


int main() {

    // Example 1: RAII

    {

        DynamicArray arr(10); // Array is
created

        // ... use the array ...

    } // Array is automatically deleted
when arr goes out of scope


    // Example 2: unique_ptr

    {

                std::unique_ptr<Widget>
widgetPtr(new Widget);
```

```cpp
    // ... use widgetPtr ...

  } // Widget is automatically deleted
when widgetPtr goes out of scope


  // Example 3: shared_ptr

  {

         std::shared_ptr<Widget>
sharedWidget(new Widget);

      processWidget(sharedWidget); //
Pass the shared_ptr to a function

     // ... sharedWidget still owns the
Widget ...

      } // Widget is deleted when
sharedWidget goes out of scope


  return 0;

}
```

## Explanation:

- **Example 1:** The DynamicArray class demonstrates RAII. The constructor allocates the array, and the destructor deallocates it. This ensures that the array is always properly deleted, even if exceptions occur.
- **Example 2:** std::unique_ptr manages the Widget object's lifetime. When widgetPtr goes out of scope, the Widget is automatically deleted.
- **Example 3:** std::shared_ptr allows shared ownership of the Widget. The processWidget function can use the Widget without worrying about its deletion. The Widget is deleted only when all shared_ptrs pointing to it go out of scope.

These code samples illustrate how to use RAII and smart pointers effectively for memory management in C++. By incorporating these techniques into your GUI applications, you can write safer, more reliable, and more maintainable code.

## Practice: Implementing simple classes and objects

To solidify your understanding of classes and objects, let's work through some practical exercises. These exercises will guide you through defining classes, creating objects, and interacting with their members.

**Exercise 1: Rectangle Class**

1. **Define a class named** Rectangle **with the following members:**
   ○ **Data members:**
      ■ width (double)
      ■ height (double)
   ○ **Member functions:**
      ■ setDimensions(double w, double h): Sets the width and height of the rectangle.
      ■ getArea(): Calculates and returns the area of the rectangle.
      ■ getPerimeter(): Calculates and returns the perimeter of the rectangle.
2. **Create an object of the** Rectangle **class.**
3. **Set the dimensions of the rectangle using the** setDimensions() **function.**
4. **Calculate and print the area and perimeter of the rectangle using the** getArea() **and** getPerimeter() **functions.**

**Solution:**

C++

#include <iostream>

```cpp
class Rectangle {
public:
    double width;
    double height;

    void setDimensions(double w, double h) {
        width = w;
        height = h;
    }

    double getArea() {
        return width * height;
    }

    double getPerimeter() {
```

```cpp
        return 2 * (width + height);

    }

};


int main() {

    Rectangle rect;

    rect.setDimensions(5.0, 3.0);


    std::cout << "Area: " << rect.getArea() << std::endl;

        std::cout << "Perimeter: " << rect.getPerimeter() << std::endl;


    return 0;

}
```

## Exercise 2: Bank Account Class

1. **Define a class named** BankAccount **with the following members:**
   - **Data members:**
     - accountNumber (int)
     - balance (double)
   - **Member functions:**
     - deposit(double amount): Adds the given amount to the balance.
     - withdraw(double amount): Subtracts the given amount from the balance,[1] if sufficient funds are available.
     - getBalance(): Returns the current balance.
2. **Create an object of the** BankAccount **class.**
3. **Deposit some initial amount into the account.**
4. **Withdraw an amount from the account.**
5. **Print the final balance.**

**Solution:**

C++

```
#include <iostream>


class BankAccount {
```

```
public:
    int accountNumber;
    double balance;

    void deposit(double amount) {
        balance += amount;
    }

    bool withdraw(double amount) {
        if (balance >= amount) {
            balance -= amount;
            return true;
        } else {
            return false; // Insufficient funds
        }
    }
```

```cpp
    double getBalance() {

        return balance;

    }

};


int main() {

    BankAccount account;

    account.accountNumber = 12345;

    account.balance = 0.0;


    account.deposit(1000.0);


    if (account.withdraw(500.0)) {

        std::cout << "Withdrawal successful." << std::endl;

    } else {
```

```cpp
        std::cout << "Insufficient funds." << std::endl;

    }



        std::cout << "Current balance: " <<
account.getBalance() << std::endl;



    return 0;

}
```

These exercises provide a basic introduction to implementing classes and objects in C++. As you progress through the book, you'll encounter more complex examples and learn how to apply these concepts to build real-world GUI applications.

# Chapter 3: Event-Driven Programming

## Understanding Events and Event Handlers

GUI programs are fundamentally different from traditional, linear programs. Instead of following a predetermined sequence of instructions, they are **event-driven**. This means they react to events triggered by the user or the system. Think of it like this: your GUI application is patiently waiting for something to happen, and when it does, it springs into action to respond appropriately.

### 1. What are Events?

In the context of GUI programming, events are actions or occurrences that happen within the application's environment. These can be triggered by various sources:

- **User Interactions:** Mouse clicks, key presses, mouse movements, window resizing, etc.
- **System Signals:** Timer expirations, network activity, hardware changes, etc.
- **Programmatic Events:** Events generated by the application itself, such as data updates or internal state changes.

**Examples of common GUI events:**

- wxEVT_BUTTON **(wxWidgets):** Generated when a button is clicked.
- clicked() **(Qt):** A signal emitted when a button is clicked.
- wxEVT_MOTION **(wxWidgets):** Generated when the mouse moves over a window or widget.
- mouseMoveEvent() **(Qt):** An event handler for mouse movement events.
- wxEVT_CLOSE_WINDOW **(wxWidgets):** Generated when a window is about to close.
- closeEvent() **(Qt):** An event handler for window closing events.

## 2. Event Handlers

Event handlers are functions or methods designed to respond to specific events. They contain the code that should be executed when a particular event occurs.

### How Event Handlers Work:

1. **Event Generation:** When an event occurs (e.g., a button click), the GUI framework detects it and creates an event object containing information about the event (e.g., which button was clicked, the mouse position).
2. **Event Dispatch:** The framework dispatches the event object to the appropriate event handler. This involves determining which part of the

application should handle the event (e.g., which button's onClick handler should be called).

3. **Event Handling:** The event handler receives the event object and executes its code, performing the necessary actions in response to the event (e.g., updating the UI, performing a calculation, sending data over the network).

**Example (Conceptual):**

C++

```cpp
// Event handler for a button click

void onButtonClicked(Event event) {

    // 1. Get information about the event (e.g., which button was clicked)

    Button clickedButton = event.getButton();


    // 2. Perform actions in response to the event

    if (clickedButton == okButton) {

        // Close the dialog

    } else if (clickedButton == cancelButton) {

        // Do something else
```

}

}

## 3. Connecting Events and Event Handlers

GUI frameworks provide mechanisms to connect events with their corresponding handlers. This typically involves:

- **Identifying the event source:** The widget or component that generates the event (e.g., a button, a window).
- **Specifying the event type:** The type of event to listen for (e.g., click, mouse move).
- **Associating the event handler:** Connecting the event to the function or method that will handle it.

**Methods for connecting events and handlers:**

- **Direct connections (Qt):** Connecting signals (events) to slots (handlers) using QObject::connect().
- **Event tables (wxWidgets):** Using macros to map events to handler functions within a class.
- **Callback functions:** Passing function pointers to widgets to be called when events occur.

## 4. The Event Loop

GUI applications typically run an **event loop**. This is a continuous cycle that:

1. **Waits for events:** The application waits for user input, system signals, or other events.
2. **Dispatches events:** When an event occurs, the event loop dispatches it to the appropriate event handler.
3. **Processes events:** The event handler executes its code in response to the event.

This event-driven model allows GUI applications to be responsive and interactive, providing a dynamic user experience. By understanding events, event handlers, and the event loop, you'll be well-equipped to build interactive and engaging GUI applications with C++, wxWidgets, and Qt.

## Signals and Slots (Qt)

Qt's signals and slots mechanism is a powerful and elegant way to handle events and communication between objects in your GUI applications. It provides a type-safe and flexible approach to connecting events with their corresponding actions, making your code cleaner and easier to maintain.

## 1. Signals

Signals are emitted by Qt objects when a particular event occurs. For example, a button emits a clicked() signal when it's clicked, and a slider emits a valueChanged() signal when its value is changed.

- **Predefined Signals:** Qt widgets come with many predefined signals for common events.
- **Custom Signals:** You can define your own signals in your custom classes to signal specific events or state changes.

## 2. Slots

Slots are normal C++ member functions that can be connected to signals. When a signal is emitted, the connected slots are called automatically.

- **Predefined Slots:** Qt widgets also have predefined slots for common actions.
- **Custom Slots:** You can define your own slots to handle specific signals.

## 3. Connecting Signals and Slots

The QObject::connect() function is used to connect a signal to a slot.

C++

```
QObject::connect(sender, &Sender::signalName, receiver, &Receiver::slotName);
```

- **sender:** The object that emits the signal.
- **&Sender::signalName:** A pointer to the signal.
- **receiver:** The object that has the slot.
- **&Receiver::slotName:** A pointer to the slot.

**Example:**

C++

```
#include <QApplication>

#include <QPushButton>

#include <QLabel>


int main(int argc, char *argv[]) {

    QApplication app(argc, argv);


    QPushButton button("Click me!");

    QLabel label("Hello!");


    // Connect the button's clicked() signal to the label's
clear() slot
```

```cpp
QObject::connect(&button, &QPushButton::clicked,
&label, &QLabel::clear);


button.show();

label.show();


return app.exec();

}
```

In this example, when the button is clicked, it emits the clicked() signal. This signal is connected to the clear() slot of the label, which clears the label's text.

### 4. Benefits of Signals and Slots

- **Type-Safety:** The compiler checks the types of the signal and slot arguments, ensuring that they are compatible.
- **Loose Coupling:** The sender and receiver objects don't need to know about each other's internal implementation.
- **Flexibility:** You can connect multiple signals to a single slot, or a single signal to multiple slots.

- **Code Reusability:** Slots can be reused to handle signals from different objects.

## 5. Advanced Concepts

- **Custom Signals and Slots:** You can define your own signals and slots in your custom classes to handle specific events.
- **Lambda Expressions:** You can use lambda expressions as slots for more concise code.
- **Qt's Meta-Object System:** Signals and slots are implemented using Qt's meta-object system, which provides introspection and dynamic properties.

Signals and slots are a fundamental part of Qt's event handling system. By mastering this mechanism, you can write efficient, maintainable, and responsive GUI applications with ease.

## Event Tables (wxWidgets)

wxWidgets uses a mechanism called **event tables** to connect events with their corresponding handler functions. This approach relies on macros to define static mappings between event types and handlers at compile time. While it might seem a bit "old-school" compared to Qt's signals and slots, event tables are efficient and straightforward, especially for simpler applications.

## 1. Declaring an Event Table

To use event tables, you need to declare an event table macro within the class where you want to handle events. This class must derive from wxEvtHandler, which is the base class for all objects that can handle events.

C++

```cpp
class MyFrame : public wxFrame {
public:
    // ... constructor and other members ...


private:
    // Event handler functions
    void OnButtonClicked(wxCommandEvent& event);

    void OnWindowClose(wxCloseEvent& event);


    wxDECLARE_EVENT_TABLE(); // Declare the event table
};
```

## 2. Defining the Event Table

Outside the class definition, you define the event table using wxBEGIN_EVENT_TABLE and wxEND_EVENT_TABLE. Inside the table, you use event macros to connect events with their handlers.

C++

```
wxBEGIN_EVENT_TABLE(MyFrame, wxFrame)

                    EVT_BUTTON(buttonId,
MyFrame::OnButtonClicked) // Connect button click to
OnButtonClicked

        EVT_CLOSE(MyFrame::OnWindowClose)   //
Connect window close to OnWindowClose

wxEND_EVENT_TABLE()
```

- wxBEGIN_EVENT_TABLE(MyFrame, wxFrame): Specifies the class (MyFrame) and its base class (wxFrame) for the event table.
- EVT_BUTTON(buttonId, MyFrame::OnButtonClicked): Connects the wxEVT_BUTTON event from the button with the specified ID (buttonId) to the OnButtonClicked handler function.

- EVT_CLOSE(MyFrame::OnWindowClose): Connects the wxEVT_CLOSE_WINDOW event to the OnWindowClose handler function.

## 3. Event Handler Functions

Event handler functions are regular member functions that take an event object as a parameter. This object contains information about the event, such as the event type, the source of the event, and any relevant data.

C++

```cpp
void MyFrame::OnButtonClicked(wxCommandEvent& event) {

    // Access event information (e.g., event.GetId() to get the button ID)

    // ... perform actions in response to the button click ...

}


void MyFrame::OnWindowClose(wxCloseEvent& event) {

    // ... perform actions before the window closes (e.g., save data) ...
```

```
    event.Skip(); // Allow the default window closing
behavior

}
```

## 4. Event Macros

wxWidgets provides a wide range of event macros for different event types. Here are a few examples:

- EVT_BUTTON: Button click.
- EVT_MENU: Menu item selection.
- EVT_TEXT: Text entered in a text control.
- EVT_CHECKBOX: Checkbox state change.
- EVT_LIST_ITEM_SELECTED: List item selection.
- EVT_TIMER: Timer expiration.

You can find a complete list of event macros in the wxWidgets documentation.

## 5. Dynamic Event Handling

While event tables are statically defined at compile time, wxWidgets also supports dynamic event handling using the Bind() method. This allows you to connect and disconnect event handlers at runtime, providing more flexibility.

C++

```
// Dynamically bind a button click to a lambda
expression

button->Bind(wxEVT_BUTTON,
[](wxCommandEvent& event){

  // ... handle the button click ...

});
```

**Benefits of Event Tables:**

- **Simple and straightforward:** Easy to understand and use, especially for beginners.
- **Efficient:** Compile-time binding can be more efficient than dynamic binding.
- **Code organization:** Keeps event handling code organized within the class.

Event tables are a core part of wxWidgets' event handling system. By understanding how to declare, define, and use event tables, you can effectively handle user interactions and build responsive GUI applications with wxWidgets.

# User Input Handling: Mouse, Keyboard, and Timers

GUI applications are all about user interaction. They need to respond to a variety of inputs, from mouse clicks and movements to keyboard presses and even the passage of time. This section explores how to handle these common types of user input in your C++ GUI applications.

## 1. Mouse Input

Mouse input typically involves handling events like:

- **Clicks:** Detecting when a mouse button is pressed and released (left-click, right-click, middle-click).
- **Movement:** Tracking the mouse cursor's position within a window or over specific widgets.
- **Dragging:** Responding to mouse movements while a button is held down.
- **Scrolling:** Handling mouse wheel events for scrolling content.

**Example (wxWidgets):**

C++

// In your frame or panel class:

```cpp
void MyPanel::OnMouseClick(wxMouseEvent& event)
{
    if (event.LeftDown()) {
        // Handle left button click
            wxPoint pos = event.GetPosition(); // Get mouse click position
        // ...
    } else if (event.RightDown()) {
        // Handle right button click
    }
}


void MyPanel::OnMouseMove(wxMouseEvent& event)
{
    wxPoint pos = event.GetPosition();
    // ... update something based on mouse position ...
}


// In your event table:
```

```
wxBEGIN_EVENT_TABLE(MyPanel, wxPanel)

  EVT_LEFT_DOWN(MyPanel::OnMouseClick)

  EVT_RIGHT_DOWN(MyPanel::OnMouseClick)

  EVT_MOTION(MyPanel::OnMouseMove)

wxEND_EVENT_TABLE()
```

**Example (Qt):**

C++

```cpp
// In your widget class:
void        MyWidget::mousePressEvent(QMouseEvent
*event) {
  if (event->button() == Qt::LeftButton) {
    // Handle left button click
        QPoint pos = event->pos(); // Get mouse click
position
    // ...
  }
}
```

```cpp
void       MyWidget::mouseMoveEvent(QMouseEvent
*event) {

    QPoint pos = event->pos();

    // ... update something based on mouse position ...

}
```

## 2. Keyboard Input

Keyboard input involves capturing key presses and releases. You might need to:

- **Respond to specific keys:** Handle individual key presses (e.g., Enter, Esc, arrow keys).
- **Process key combinations:** Detect shortcuts (e.g., Ctrl+S for save, Ctrl+C for copy).
- **Handle text input:** Capture characters typed into text fields.

**Example (wxWidgets):**

C++

```cpp
void MyFrame::OnKeyDown(wxKeyEvent& event) {

    int keycode = event.GetKeyCode();
```

```
if (keycode == WXK_ESCAPE) {

    // Handle Escape key press

    Close();

} else if (event.ControlDown() && keycode == 'S') {

    // Handle Ctrl+S

    // ... save data ...

}

    event.Skip(); // Allow other handlers to process the
event

}


// In your event table:

wxBEGIN_EVENT_TABLE(MyFrame, wxFrame)

    EVT_KEY_DOWN(MyFrame::OnKeyDown)

wxEND_EVENT_TABLE()
```

**Example (Qt):**

C++

```
void MyWidget::keyPressEvent(QKeyEvent *event) {

    if (event->key() == Qt::Key_Escape) {

        // Handle Escape key press

        close();

    } else if (event->modifiers() == Qt::ControlModifier
&& event->key() == Qt::Key_S) {

        // Handle Ctrl+S

        // ... save data ...

    }

}
```

## 3. Timers

Timers allow you to perform actions at regular intervals
or after a specific delay. They are useful for:

- **Animation:** Updating the UI to create
  animations.
- **Progress updates:** Displaying progress bars or
  status updates.
- **Background tasks:** Performing periodic tasks in
  the background.

**Example (wxWidgets):**

C++

```cpp
// Create a timer
wxTimer timer(this, TIMER_ID);

// Start the timer (1000 milliseconds = 1 second)
timer.Start(1000);

// Event handler for timer events
void MyFrame::OnTimer(wxTimerEvent& event) {
    // ... perform periodic actions ...
}

// In your event table:
wxBEGIN_EVENT_TABLE(MyFrame, wxFrame)
    EVT_TIMER(TIMER_ID, MyFrame::OnTimer)
wxEND_EVENT_TABLE()
```

**Example (Qt):**

C++

```cpp
// Create a timer
QTimer *timer = new QTimer(this);

// Connect the timer's timeout() signal to a slot
connect(timer, &QTimer::timeout, this, &MyWidget::updateDisplay);

// Start the timer (1000 milliseconds = 1 second)
timer->start(1000);

// Slot to handle timer events
void MyWidget::updateDisplay() {
    // ... update the display ...
}
```

By effectively handling mouse, keyboard, and timer events, you can create GUI applications that are interactive, responsive, and engaging for your users. Remember to consult the documentation for wxWidgets and Qt for more details on specific event types and handling techniques.

## Code samples: Handling button clicks, mouse movements, and keyboard input

C++

```cpp
// wxWidgets Example


#include <wx/wxprec.h>

#ifndef WX_PRECOMP

    #include <wx/wx.h>

#endif


class MyFrame : public wxFrame

{

public:
```

```cpp
    MyFrame(const wxString& title, const
wxPoint& pos, const wxSize& size);

private:

    void OnButtonClicked(wxCommandEvent&
event);

    void OnMouseMove(wxMouseEvent& event);

    void OnKeyDown(wxKeyEvent& event);

    wxTextCtrl* textCtrl; // Text control
to display messages

    wxDECLARE_EVENT_TABLE();

};



wxBEGIN_EVENT_TABLE(MyFrame, wxFrame)

                        EVT_BUTTON(wxID_ANY,
MyFrame::OnButtonClicked)

    EVT_MOTION(MyFrame::OnMouseMove)

    EVT_KEY_DOWN(MyFrame::OnKeyDown)

wxEND_EVENT_TABLE()
```

```cpp
wxIMPLEMENT_APP(MyApp);


bool MyApp::OnInit()

{

    MyFrame *frame = new MyFrame( "Input
Handling",  wxPoint(50,  50),  wxSize(450,
340) );

    frame->Show( true );

    return true;

}



MyFrame::MyFrame(const   wxString&   title,
const wxPoint& pos, const wxSize& size)

            : wxFrame(NULL, wxID_ANY, title,
pos, size)

{

    wxPanel*  panel  =  new  wxPanel(this,
wxID_ANY);

    wxButton* button = new wxButton(panel,
wxID_ANY, "Click Me!", wxPoint(10, 10));
```

```cpp
        textCtrl = new wxTextCtrl(panel,
wxID_ANY, "", wxPoint(10, 50), wxSize(200,
100), wxTE_MULTILINE);

}



void
MyFrame::OnButtonClicked(wxCommandEvent&
event) {

            textCtrl->AppendText("Button
clicked!\n");

}



void    MyFrame::OnMouseMove(wxMouseEvent&
event) {

    wxPoint pos = event.GetPosition();


textCtrl->AppendText(wxString::Format("Mous
e moved to (%d, %d)\n", pos.x, pos.y));

}



void MyFrame::OnKeyDown(wxKeyEvent& event)
{
```

```cpp
    int keycode = event.GetKeyCode();

textCtrl->AppendText(wxString::Format("Key
pressed: %d\n", keycode));

        event.Skip();  //  Allow   default
processing (e.g., text input)

}
```

**C++**

```cpp
// Qt Example

#include <QApplication>

#include <QPushButton>

#include <QTextEdit>

class MyWidget : public QWidget {
    Q_OBJECT

public:
```

```cpp
    MyWidget(QWidget *parent = nullptr) :
QWidget(parent) {

            QPushButton *button = new
QPushButton("Click Me!", this);

        textEdit = new QTextEdit(this);



                        connect(button,
&QPushButton::clicked,                this,
&MyWidget::onButtonClicked);



            QVBoxLayout *layout = new
QVBoxLayout(this);

        layout->addWidget(button);

        layout->addWidget(textEdit);

    }


private slots:

    void onButtonClicked() {

                textEdit->append("Button
clicked!");
```

```cpp
    }


protected:

    void mouseMoveEvent(QMouseEvent *event) override {

        QPoint pos = event->pos();

            textEdit->append(QString("Mouse
moved             to             (%1,
%2)").arg(pos.x()).arg(pos.y()));

    }



    void keyPressEvent(QKeyEvent *event) override {

        int key = event->key();

            textEdit->append(QString("Key
pressed: %1").arg(key));

    }


private:

    QTextEdit *textEdit;
```

```
};


int main(int argc, char *argv[]) {

    QApplication app(argc, argv);

    MyWidget widget;

    widget.show();

    return app.exec();

}
```

**Explanation:**

- **wxWidgets:**
    - The MyFrame class handles button clicks (OnButtonClicked), mouse movements (OnMouseMove), and key presses (OnKeyDown).
    - The event table connects these handlers to the corresponding events.
    - The textCtrl is used to display messages about the events.
- **Qt:**
    - The MyWidget class handles button clicks (onButtonClicked), mouse

movements (mouseMoveEvent), and key presses (keyPressEvent).

- ○ The connect() function connects the button's clicked() signal to the onButtonClicked slot.
- ○ The textEdit is used to display messages about the events.

Both examples demonstrate how to capture and respond to basic user input events. You can extend these examples to create more complex interactions and build interactive GUI applications.

## Practice: Creating a simple interactive application that responds to user events

### Practice: Creating a Simple Interactive Application

**Objective:** Build a simple interactive application that responds to user events. This exercise will help you solidify your understanding of event handling and basic GUI programming concepts.

### Application Idea: A Basic Drawing Pad

Create a drawing pad application with the following features:

- A canvas area where the user can draw lines with the mouse.
- A button to clear the canvas.
- Optionally, different colors or line thicknesses for drawing.

**Implementation Guidelines:**

1. **Choose your framework:** Decide whether you want to use wxWidgets or Qt for this exercise.
2. **Create a main window:** Set up a main application window with a title.
3. **Add a drawing canvas:** Create a widget (e.g., wxPanel in wxWidgets, QWidget in Qt) to serve as the drawing canvas.
4. **Handle mouse events:**
   - **Mouse down:** Start drawing a line from the current mouse position.
   - **Mouse move:** If the mouse button is held down, continue drawing the line to the new mouse position.
   - **Mouse up:** Stop drawing the line.
5. **Add a clear button:** Create a button labeled "Clear."
6. **Handle button click:** Connect the button's click event to a function that clears the canvas.
7. **(Optional) Add color options:** Provide buttons or a menu to select different drawing colors.

8. **(Optional) Add line thickness options:** Allow the user to choose different line thicknesses.

**wxWidgets Example (Basic Structure):**

C++

```cpp
#include <wx/wxprec.h>

#ifndef WX_PRECOMP
    #include <wx/wx.h>
#endif


class MyFrame : public wxFrame
{
public:
    MyFrame(const wxString& title);


private:
    void OnMouseDown(wxMouseEvent& event);

    void OnMouseMove(wxMouseEvent& event);
```

```cpp
    void OnMouseUp(wxMouseEvent& event);

        void   OnClearButtonClicked(wxCommandEvent&
event);


    wxPanel* drawingPanel;

    bool isDrawing;

    wxPoint lastPoint;


    wxDECLARE_EVENT_TABLE();
};


// ... (Implementation of event handlers and other
functions) ...
```

**Qt Example (Basic Structure):**

```cpp
C++

#include <QtWidgets>
```

```cpp
class MyWidget : public QWidget {

    Q_OBJECT

public:

    MyWidget(QWidget *parent = nullptr);

protected:

        void mousePressEvent(QMouseEvent *event) override;

        void mouseMoveEvent(QMouseEvent *event) override;

        void mouseReleaseEvent(QMouseEvent *event) override;

private slots:

    void onClearButtonClicked();
```

```cpp
private:

    void paintEvent(QPaintEvent *event) override;


private:

    QPushButton *clearButton;

    bool isDrawing;

    QPoint lastPoint;

};



// ... (Implementation of event handlers and other functions) ...
```

This practice exercise will challenge you to apply your knowledge of event handling, user input, and basic GUI programming. Don't hesitate to experiment with different features and explore the documentation of your chosen framework for more advanced options. Good luck!

# Part II: wxWidgets Development

# Chapter 4: Introduction to wxWidgets

## Core Concepts: Frames, Panels, Widgets, Sizers

wxWidgets provides a rich set of classes and tools for building cross-platform GUI applications. To get started, it's essential to understand some of its core concepts: frames, panels, widgets, and sizers. These form the building blocks of your wxWidgets applications.

### 1. Frames (wxFrame)

A frame is a top-level window that serves as the main container for your application's user interface. It typically has a title bar, a menu bar (optional), a status bar (optional), and a client area where you place other GUI elements.

- **Creating a Frame:**

C++

```
#include <wx/wx.h>


class MyFrame : public wxFrame {
public:
    MyFrame(const wxString& title)
```

```
        : wxFrame(NULL, wxID_ANY, title) {}

};
```

- **Key methods:**
  - SetTitle(const wxString& title): Sets the frame's title.
  - SetSize(const wxSize& size): Sets the frame's size.
  - SetPosition(const wxPoint& pos): Sets the frame's position on the screen.
  - Show(bool show = true): Shows or hides the frame.
  - Close(bool force = false): Closes the frame.

## 2. Panels (wxPanel)

A panel is a container widget that holds other widgets. It acts as an intermediate container within a frame or another panel, allowing you to group and organize related widgets.

- **Creating a Panel:**

C++

```
wxPanel* panel = new wxPanel(parent, wxID_ANY); //
parent is a wxWindow, e.g., a frame
```

- **Why use Panels?**
  - ○ **Organization:** Group related widgets together.
  - ○ **Event Handling:** Handle events at the panel level.
  - ○ **Custom Drawing:** Create custom drawing areas within a panel.

## 3. Widgets

Widgets are the basic user interface elements in wxWidgets. They represent controls like buttons, text boxes, labels, checkboxes, list boxes, etc.

- **Common Widgets:**
  - ○ wxButton: A clickable button.
  - ○ wxTextCtrl: A single-line or multi-line text input field.
  - ○ wxStaticText: A non-editable text label.
  - ○ wxCheckBox: A checkbox that can be checked or unchecked.
  - ○ wxListBox: A list of selectable items.
  - ○ wxComboBox: A dropdown list of selectable items.
- **Creating a Widget:**

C++

```
wxButton* button = new wxButton(parent, wxID_ANY,
"Click Me!"); // parent is a wxWindow
```

## 4. Sizers (wxSizer)

Sizers are layout managers that control the size and position of widgets within their parent container. They allow you to create flexible and dynamic layouts that adapt to different window sizes and platform variations.

- **Types of Sizers:**
  - wxBoxSizer: Arranges widgets horizontally or vertically.
  - wxGridSizer: Arranges widgets in a grid.
  - wxFlexGridSizer: A more flexible grid sizer that can have rows and columns of different sizes.
  - wxStaticBoxSizer: A box sizer with a label around it.
- **Using Sizers:**

C++

```
wxBoxSizer* mainSizer = new
wxBoxSizer(wxVERTICAL); // Create a vertical sizer
```

```
mainSizer->Add(button, 0, wxALL, 5); // Add a button
with padding

mainSizer->Add(textCtrl, 1, wxEXPAND | wxALL, 5);
// Add a text control that expands

panel->SetSizer(mainSizer); // Set the sizer for the panel
```

- **Sizer Attributes:**
  - **Proportion:** Controls how much space a widget gets within the sizer (e.g., 0 for fixed size, 1 for expanding).
  - **Flags:** Specify alignment, borders, and other layout options (e.g., wxEXPAND, wxALIGN_CENTER, wxALL).
  - **Border:** Adds spacing around the widget.

**Putting it all together:**

Frames, panels, widgets, and sizers work together to create the user interface of your wxWidgets application. Frames provide the main window, panels help organize widgets, widgets provide the interactive elements, and sizers manage their layout. By understanding these core concepts, you can build well-structured and visually appealing GUI applications.

# Building Your First wxWidgets Application

It's time to put the core concepts into practice and build your first wxWidgets application! We'll create a simple "Hello, World!" program with a window, a button, and a text control. This will introduce you to the basic structure of a wxWidgets application and how to handle events.

## Step 1: Include the wxWidgets header

Every wxWidgets program needs to include the main header file:

C++

```
#include <wx/wxprec.h>
#ifndef WX_PRECOMP
    #include <wx/wx.h>
#endif
```

This header includes all the necessary definitions for using wxWidgets.

## Step 2: Create an application class

Every wxWidgets application needs an application class derived from wxApp. This class represents the application itself and provides an entry point for initialization.

C++

```
class MyApp : public wxApp
{
public:
    virtual bool OnInit(); // Override the OnInit function
};
```

The OnInit() function is called when the application starts. We'll override it to create our main window.

## Step 3: Create a frame class

A frame is the main window of your application. We'll create a class derived from wxFrame to represent our window.

C++

```
class MyFrame : public wxFrame
```

```cpp
{
public:

    MyFrame(const wxString& title, const wxPoint& pos,
const wxSize& size);

private:

    void OnHello(wxCommandEvent& event); // Event
handler for the button click

    wxTextCtrl* textCtrl; // Text control to display the
message

    wxDECLARE_EVENT_TABLE(); // Declare the
event table

};
```

- The constructor takes the window title, position, and size as arguments.
- OnHello() is the event handler function that will be called when the button is clicked.
- textCtrl is a pointer to a wxTextCtrl widget that will display the "Hello, World!" message.

**Step 4: Define the event table**

We'll use an event table to connect the button click event to our OnHello() handler function.

C++

```
wxBEGIN_EVENT_TABLE(MyFrame, wxFrame)

    EVT_BUTTON(wxID_ANY, MyFrame::OnHello) // Connect any button click to OnHello

wxEND_EVENT_TABLE()
```

## Step 5: Implement the application and frame classes

Now let's implement the OnInit() function in our application class and the constructor and event handler in our frame class.

C++

```
wxIMPLEMENT_APP(MyApp); // Tell wxWidgets to create an instance of MyApp


bool MyApp::OnInit()
{
```

```cpp
    MyFrame *frame = new MyFrame("Hello World",
wxPoint(50, 50), wxSize(450, 340));

    frame->Show(true);

    return true;

}


MyFrame::MyFrame(const   wxString&   title,   const
wxPoint& pos, const wxSize& size)
    : wxFrame(NULL, wxID_ANY, title, pos, size)

{

    wxPanel* panel = new wxPanel(this, wxID_ANY); //
Create a panel within the frame

        wxButton*  button  =  new  wxButton(panel,
wxID_ANY, "Say Hello", wxPoint(10, 10)); // Create a
button

        textCtrl = new wxTextCtrl(panel, wxID_ANY, "",
wxPoint(10, 50), wxSize(200, 100), wxTE_MULTILINE
| wxTE_READONLY); // Create a text control

}


void MyFrame::OnHello(wxCommandEvent& event) {
```

```
textCtrl->AppendText("Hello, world!\n");

}
```

- MyApp::OnInit(): Creates an instance of MyFrame and shows it.
- MyFrame::MyFrame(): Creates a panel, a button, and a text control within the frame.
- MyFrame::OnHello(): Appends "Hello, world!" to the text control.

**Step 6: Compile and run**

Compile your code using a C++ compiler and link it with the wxWidgets library. When you run the application, you should see a window with a button labeled "Say Hello". Clicking the button will display "Hello, world!" in the text control.

Congratulations! You've built your first wxWidgets application. This simple example demonstrates the basic structure and event handling in wxWidgets. You can now expand on this foundation to create more complex and interactive GUI applications.

# Step-by-step guide to creating a basic window with controls

let's break down the process of creating a basic window with controls in wxWidgets, step-by-step.

## Step 1: Create the basic application structure

This involves setting up the wxApp and wxFrame classes, as we did in the previous "Hello, World!" example.

C++

```cpp
#include <wx/wxprec.h>

#ifndef WX_PRECOMP
    #include <wx/wx.h>
#endif


class MyApp : public wxApp
{
public:
```

```cpp
    virtual bool OnInit();

};


class MyFrame : public wxFrame

{

public:

    MyFrame(const wxString& title, const wxPoint& pos,
const wxSize& size);

private:

    wxDECLARE_EVENT_TABLE();

};


wxBEGIN_EVENT_TABLE(MyFrame, wxFrame)

// We'll add event handlers here later

wxEND_EVENT_TABLE()


wxIMPLEMENT_APP(MyApp);
```

```cpp
bool MyApp::OnInit()

{

    MyFrame *frame = new MyFrame("Basic Window",
wxPoint(50, 50), wxSize(450, 340));

    frame->Show(true);

    return true;

}
```

## Step 2: Add a panel to the frame

A wxPanel acts as a container for other widgets. We'll add one to our frame's client area.

C++

```cpp
MyFrame::MyFrame(const    wxString&    title,    const
wxPoint& pos, const wxSize& size)

    : wxFrame(NULL, wxID_ANY, title, pos, size)

{
```

```cpp
    wxPanel* panel = new wxPanel(this, wxID_ANY); //
Create a panel with the frame as its parent

    // ... we'll add controls to this panel in the next steps ...

}
```

## Step 3: Add controls to the panel

Let's add some common controls: a button, a text control, and a static text label.

C++

```cpp
MyFrame::MyFrame(const    wxString&    title,    const
wxPoint& pos, const wxSize& size)

      : wxFrame(NULL, wxID_ANY, title, pos, size)

{

    wxPanel* panel = new wxPanel(this, wxID_ANY);



        wxButton*    button   =   new   wxButton(panel,
wxID_ANY, "Click Me!", wxPoint(10, 10));
```

```
    wxTextCtrl* textCtrl = new wxTextCtrl(panel,
wxID_ANY, "", wxPoint(10, 50), wxSize(200, 30));

    wxStaticText* staticText = new wxStaticText(panel,
wxID_ANY, "Enter some text:", wxPoint(10, 90));

}
```

## Step 4: Arrange the controls with a sizer

We'll use a wxBoxSizer to arrange the controls vertically.

C++

```
MyFrame::MyFrame(const    wxString&    title,    const
wxPoint& pos, const wxSize& size)

    : wxFrame(NULL, wxID_ANY, title, pos, size)

{

  wxPanel* panel = new wxPanel(this, wxID_ANY);


  // ... (controls from the previous step) ...
```

```cpp
    wxBoxSizer*    sizer    =    new wxBoxSizer(wxVERTICAL);

    sizer->Add(button, 0, wxALL, 5); // Add button with 5px padding on all sides

    sizer->Add(textCtrl, 0, wxALL, 5); // Add text control with padding

    sizer->Add(staticText, 0, wxALL, 5); // Add static text with padding

    panel->SetSizer(sizer); // Set the sizer for the panel

}
```

**Step 5: (Optional) Add an event handler**

Let's add an event handler to the button to show a message box when it's clicked.

C++

```cpp
// ... (previous code) ...


private:
```

```cpp
void OnButtonClicked(wxCommandEvent& event);
```

```
// ... (in the event table) ...
```

```
                    EVT_BUTTON(wxID_ANY,
MyFrame::OnButtonClicked)
```

```
// ... (implementation) ...
```

```cpp
void MyFrame::OnButtonClicked(wxCommandEvent&
event) {

    wxMessageBox("Button clicked!", "Message", wxOK
| wxICON_INFORMATION);

}
```

### Step 6: Compile and run

Compile and run your application. You should now see a window with a button, a text control, and a static text label, all neatly arranged. Clicking the button will display a message box.

This step-by-step guide shows you how to create a basic window with controls in wxWidgets. You can now experiment with different controls, sizers, and event handlers to build more complex and interactive GUI applications.

## Code samples: A simple note-taking application with menus and a text area

C++

```cpp
#include <wx/wxprec.h>

#ifndef WX_PRECOMP
    #include <wx/wx.h>
#endif


#include <wx/filedlg.h> // For file dialogs


class MyApp : public wxApp
{
public:
    virtual bool OnInit();
```

```cpp
};


class MyFrame : public wxFrame

{

public:

    MyFrame(const wxString& title, const
wxPoint& pos, const wxSize& size);


private:

    void OnNew(wxCommandEvent& event);

    void OnOpen(wxCommandEvent& event);

    void OnSave(wxCommandEvent& event);

    void OnExit(wxCommandEvent& event);

    void OnAbout(wxCommandEvent& event);


    wxTextCtrl* textArea;

    wxString currentFilename; // To store
the current file name
```

```cpp
    wxDECLARE_EVENT_TABLE();
};


enum
{
    ID_New = 1,
    ID_Open,
    ID_Save,
    ID_Exit,
    ID_About
};


wxBEGIN_EVENT_TABLE(MyFrame, wxFrame)
    EVT_MENU(ID_New, MyFrame::OnNew)
    EVT_MENU(ID_Open, MyFrame::OnOpen)
    EVT_MENU(ID_Save, MyFrame::OnSave)
    EVT_MENU(ID_Exit, MyFrame::OnExit)
    EVT_MENU(ID_About, MyFrame::OnAbout)
```

```cpp
wxEND_EVENT_TABLE()


wxIMPLEMENT_APP(MyApp);


bool MyApp::OnInit()
{
    MyFrame *frame = new MyFrame("Notepad",
wxPoint(50, 50), wxSize(800, 600));

    frame->Show(true);

    return true;

}



MyFrame::MyFrame(const    wxString&    title,
const wxPoint& pos, const wxSize& size)

            : wxFrame(NULL, wxID_ANY, title,
pos, size)
{
    // Create menu bar

    wxMenu *menuFile = new wxMenu;
```

```
                    menuFile->Append(ID_New,
"&New\tCtrl-N");

                     menuFile->Append(ID_Open,
"&Open\tCtrl-O");

                     menuFile->Append(ID_Save,
"&Save\tCtrl-S");

    menuFile->AppendSeparator();

    menuFile->Append(ID_Exit);


    wxMenu *menuHelp = new wxMenu;

    menuHelp->Append(ID_About);


    wxMenuBar *menuBar = new wxMenuBar;

    menuBar->Append(menuFile, "&File");

    menuBar->Append(menuHelp, "&Help");

    SetMenuBar(menuBar);


    // Create text area
```

```cpp
    textArea = new wxTextCtrl(this,
wxID_ANY, "", wxDefaultPosition,
wxDefaultSize, wxTE_MULTILINE);

}




void MyFrame::OnNew(wxCommandEvent& event)
{

    textArea->Clear();

    currentFilename = "";

}




void MyFrame::OnOpen(wxCommandEvent& event)
{

    wxFileDialog openFileDialog(this,
_("Open File"), "", "",

                            "Text files
(*.txt)|*.txt", wxFD_OPEN |
wxFD_FILE_MUST_EXIST);

    if (openFileDialog.ShowModal() ==
wxID_CANCEL)

        return;
```

```
                    currentFilename        =
openFileDialog.GetPath();

                                              if
(!textArea->LoadFile(currentFilename)) {

            wxLogError("Cannot  open  file
'%s'.", currentFilename);

        return;

    }

}



void MyFrame::OnSave(wxCommandEvent& event)
{

    if (currentFilename.empty()) {

            wxFileDialog saveFileDialog(this,
_("Save File"), "", "",

                                        "Text
files    (*.txt)|*.txt",    wxFD_SAVE    |
wxFD_OVERWRITE_PROMPT);

            if (saveFileDialog.ShowModal() ==
wxID_CANCEL)
```

```cpp
        return;

            currentFilename   =
saveFileDialog.GetPath();

    }

                        if
(!textArea->SaveFile(currentFilename)) {

        wxLogError("Cannot save current
contents in file '%s'.", currentFilename);

        return;

    }

}


void MyFrame::OnExit(wxCommandEvent& event)
{

    Close(true);

}


void         MyFrame::OnAbout(wxCommandEvent&
event) {
```

```
                    wxMessageBox("Simple     Notepad
Application\nUsing wxWidgets",

                         "About Notepad", wxOK |
wxICON_INFORMATION);

}
```

This code creates a basic notepad application with a menu bar (File and Help menus), and a multi-line text area. The File menu has options for New, Open, and Save, allowing users to create, open, and save text files. The Help menu has an About option that displays information about the application. The application demonstrates how to use menus, file dialogs, and basic file I/O in wxWidgets.

## Practice: Modifying the application to add more features

Let's take your notepad application to the next level by adding some useful features. Here are a few ideas to get you started:

### 1. Font Selection

- Add a "Format" menu to the menu bar.
- Include a "Font..." menu item that opens a font selection dialog (wxFontDialog).

- Allow the user to choose a font family, style (bold, italic), size, and color.
- Apply the selected font to the text area.

## 2. Word Count

- Add a "View" menu to the menu bar.
- Include a "Word Count" menu item.
- When this item is selected, display a message box showing the number of words in the text area.
- You can use wxString::Split() to split the text into words.

## 3. Find and Replace

- Add an "Edit" menu to the menu bar.
- Include "Find..." and "Replace..." menu items.
- Create dialogs for finding and replacing text within the text area.
- Use wxTextCtrl::Find() to locate text and wxTextCtrl::Replace() to replace it.

## 4. Line Numbers

- Add an option in the "View" menu to toggle line numbers on and off.
- When line numbers are enabled, display them in a separate area next to the text area.
- You might need to use a more advanced layout mechanism like wxGridSizer to achieve this.

## 5. Printing

- Add a "Print..." menu item to the "File" menu.
- Use the wxPrintDialog and wxPrintout classes to implement printing functionality.

## 6. Syntax Highlighting (Advanced)

- If you're feeling ambitious, try adding syntax highlighting for a specific programming language (e.g., C++, Python).
- This involves analyzing the text and applying different colors and styles to keywords, comments, and other language elements.
- You might need to use a more advanced text control like wxStyledTextCtrl for this.

## Example: Adding Font Selection

C++

```
// ... (In MyFrame class) ...


void MyFrame::OnFont(wxCommandEvent& event) {

    wxFontData data;

    data.EnableEffects(true);
```

```cpp
    wxFontDialog dialog(this, data);

    if (dialog.ShowModal() == wxID_OK) {

        wxFontData retData = dialog.GetFontData();

        wxFont font = retData.GetChosenFont();

        textArea->SetFont(font);

    }

}


// ... (In the event table) ...

    EVT_MENU(ID_Font, MyFrame::OnFont)


// ... (In the menu bar creation) ...

    wxMenu *menuFormat = new wxMenu;

    menuFormat->Append(ID_Font, "Font...");

    menuBar->Append(menuFormat, "&Format");
```

Remember to consult the wxWidgets documentation for details on the classes and methods you'll need for each feature. This practice will help you gain experience with wxWidgets and build more complex and functional GUI applications.

# Chapter 5: Working with wxWidgets Controls

## Basic Controls: Buttons, Text Boxes, Labels, Checkboxes, Radio Buttons

wxWidgets offers a wide array of controls for building user interfaces. In this section, we'll explore some of the most fundamental controls: buttons, text boxes, labels, checkboxes, and radio buttons. You'll learn how to create them, configure their properties, and handle their events.

**1. Buttons** (wxButton)

Buttons are essential for triggering actions in your application. They can be labeled with text, icons, or both.

- **Creation:**

C++

```
wxButton* button = new wxButton(parent, id, label, position, size, style);
```

- **Common parameters:**
  - parent: The parent window or panel.

- id: An identifier for the button (e.g., wxID_ANY, ID_OK, ID_CANCEL).
- label: The text displayed on the button.
- position: The button's position within the parent.
- size: The button's size.
- style: Button styles (e.g., wxBU_LEFT, wxBU_RIGHT, wxBU_TOP, wxBU_BOTTOM for label alignment).

- **Event handling:**
  - EVT_BUTTON(id, handler): Connects the button's click event to the specified handler function.

## 2. Text Boxes (wxTextCtrl)

Text boxes allow users to enter and edit text. They can be single-line or multi-line.

- **Creation:**

C++

```
wxTextCtrl* textCtrl = new wxTextCtrl(parent, id, value, position, size, style);
```

- **Common parameters:**
  - value: The initial text in the text box.

- style: Text box styles (e.g., wxTE_MULTILINE, wxTE_PASSWORD, wxTE_READONLY).
- **Key methods:**
  - GetValue(): Gets the text in the text box.
  - SetValue(const wxString& value): Sets the text in the text box.
  - AppendText(const wxString& text): Appends text to the end.
  - Clear(): Clears the text.
- **Event handling:**
  - EVT_TEXT(id, handler): Generated when the text changes.
  - EVT_TEXT_ENTER(id, handler): Generated when Enter is pressed in the text box.

## 3. Labels (wxStaticText)

Labels display static text that cannot be edited by the user.

- **Creation:**

C++

```
wxStaticText* staticText = new wxStaticText(parent, id, label, position, size, style);
```

- **Common parameters:**
  - style: Label styles (e.g., wxALIGN_LEFT, wxALIGN_CENTER, wxALIGN_RIGHT).
- **Key methods:**
  - SetLabel(const wxString& label): Sets the label's text.

## 4. Checkboxes (wxCheckBox)

Checkboxes allow users to select or deselect an option.

- **Creation:**

C++

```
wxCheckBox* checkBox = new wxCheckBox(parent, id, label, position, size, style);
```

- **Key methods:**
  - GetValue(): Gets the checkbox state (true if checked, false if unchecked).
  - SetValue(bool checked): Sets the checkbox state.
- **Event handling:**

- EVT_CHECKBOX(id, handler): Generated when the checkbox state changes.

## 5. Radio Buttons (wxRadioButton)

Radio buttons allow users to select one option from a group of mutually exclusive options.

- **Creation:**

C++

```
wxRadioButton*          radioButton          =          new
wxRadioButton(parent, id, label, position, size, style);
```

- **Common parameters:**
  - style: Radio button styles (e.g., wxRB_GROUP to start a new group).
- **Key methods:**
  - GetValue(): Gets the radio button state.
  - SetValue(bool selected): Sets the radio button state.
- **Event handling:**
  - EVT_RADIOBUTTON(id, handler): Generated when the radio button state changes.

**Example:**

C++

```cpp
// ... (In your frame or panel constructor) ...


wxButton* button = new wxButton(panel, wxID_ANY, "Submit");

wxTextCtrl* nameText = new wxTextCtrl(panel, wxID_ANY, "");

wxStaticText* nameLabel = new wxStaticText(panel, wxID_ANY, "Name:");

wxCheckBox* subscribeCheck = new wxCheckBox(panel, wxID_ANY, "Subscribe to newsletter");


wxRadioButton* maleRadio = new wxRadioButton(panel, wxID_ANY, "Male", wxDefaultPosition, wxDefaultSize, wxRB_GROUP);

wxRadioButton* femaleRadio = new wxRadioButton(panel, wxID_ANY, "Female");


// ... (Add controls to a sizer for proper layout) ...
```

This example demonstrates how to create and use basic controls in wxWidgets. You can combine these controls with sizers and event handlers to create interactive and functional user interfaces.

## Advanced Controls: List Controls, Tree Controls, Grids

Beyond the basic controls, wxWidgets provides more complex and powerful controls for handling lists of items, hierarchical data, and tabular information. These advanced controls offer greater flexibility and functionality for your GUI applications.

**1. List Controls** (wxListCtrl)

List controls display collections of items in various formats:

- **List view:** Items are displayed in a vertical list with optional icons.
- **Report view:** Items are displayed in a tabular format with columns and headings.
- **Icon view:** Items are displayed as icons with labels.
- **Small icon view:** Similar to icon view, but with smaller icons.

- **Creation:**

C++

wxListCtrl* listCtrl = new wxListCtrl(parent, id, position, size, style);

- **Common styles:**
    - wxLC_LIST: List view.
    - wxLC_REPORT: Report view.
    - wxLC_ICON: Icon view.
    - wxLC_SMALL_ICON: Small icon view.
    - wxLC_SINGLE_SEL: Single selection.
    - wxLC_MULTIPLE_SEL: Multiple selection.
- **Key methods (Report view):**
    - InsertColumn(long col, const wxListItem& item): Inserts a column.
    - InsertItem(long index, const wxListItem& item): Inserts an item.
    - SetItem(const wxListItem& item): Sets the properties of an item.
    - GetItemCount(): Gets the number of items.
    - GetSelectedItemCount(): Gets the number of selected items.
- **Event handling:**

- EVT_LIST_ITEM_SELECTED(id, handler): Generated when an item is selected.
- EVT_LIST_ITEM_DESELECTED(id, handler): Generated when an item is deselected.
- EVT_LIST_ITEM_ACTIVATED(id, handler): Generated when an item is activated (e.g., double-clicked).

## 2. Tree Controls (wxTreeCtrl)

Tree controls display hierarchical data in a tree-like structure with expandable and collapsible nodes.

- **Creation:**

C++

```
wxTreeCtrl* treeCtrl = new wxTreeCtrl(parent, id, position, size, style);
```

- **Key methods:**
  - AddRoot(const wxString& text): Adds the root node.
  - AppendItem(const wxTreeItemId& parent, const wxString& text): Appends a child item to a parent.

- Expand(const wxTreeItemId& item): Expands a node.
- Collapse(const wxTreeItemId& item): Collapses a node.
- GetSelection(): Gets the selected item.
- **Event handling:**
  - EVT_TREE_SEL_CHANGED(id, handler): Generated when the selection changes.
  - EVT_TREE_ITEM_EXPANDING(id, handler): Generated when a node is about to expand.
  - EVT_TREE_ITEM_EXPANDED(id, handler): Generated when a node has been expanded.
  - EVT_TREE_ITEM_ACTIVATED(id, handler): Generated when an item is activated.

## 3. Grids (wxGrid)

Grids display data in a tabular format with rows and columns, similar to a spreadsheet.

- **Creation:**

C++

```
wxGrid* grid = new wxGrid(parent, id, position, size, style);
```

- **Key methods:**
  - CreateGrid(int numRows, int numCols): Creates the grid with the specified number of rows and columns.
  - SetCellValue(int row, int col, const wxString& value): Sets the value of a cell.
  - GetCellValue(int row, int col): Gets the value of a cell.
  - SetColLabelValue(int col, const wxString& value): Sets the label of a column.
  - SetRowLabelValue(int row, const wxString& value): Sets the label of a row.
- **Event handling:**
  - EVT_GRID_CELL_LEFT_CLICK(id, handler): Generated when a cell is left-clicked.
  - EVT_GRID_CELL_RIGHT_CLICK(id, handler): Generated when a cell is right-clicked.
  - EVT_GRID_CELL_CHANGING(id, handler): Generated when a cell's value is about to change.

- o EVT_GRID_CELL_CHANGED(id, handler): Generated when a cell's value has changed.

By utilizing these advanced controls, you can create more sophisticated and data-rich user interfaces in your wxWidgets applications. They provide powerful ways to present and interact with complex information, enhancing the functionality and user experience of your programs.

## Layout Management with Sizers: BoxSizer, GridSizer, FlexGridSizer

Sizers are the key to creating well-organized and adaptable layouts in wxWidgets. They manage the size and position of your widgets, ensuring they look good and behave correctly regardless of the window size or platform. Let's explore three essential sizer types: wxBoxSizer, wxGridSizer, and wxFlexGridSizer.

**1.** wxBoxSizer

wxBoxSizer is the most common and versatile sizer. It arranges widgets in a horizontal or vertical line.

- **Creation:**

C++

```cpp
wxBoxSizer* sizer = new wxBoxSizer(orientation);
```

- orientation: wxHORIZONTAL or wxVERTICAL.
- **Adding widgets:**

C++

```cpp
sizer->Add(widget, proportion, flags, border);
```

- widget: The widget to add.
- proportion: How much space the widget should take relative to other widgets in the sizer (0 for fixed size, 1 for expanding to fill available space).
- flags: Layout options (e.g., wxEXPAND, wxALIGN_CENTER, wxALL).
- border: Spacing around the widget.
- **Example:**

C++

```cpp
wxBoxSizer* hSizer = new wxBoxSizer(wxHORIZONTAL);
```

```cpp
hSizer->Add(button1, 1, wxEXPAND | wxALL, 5); //
Expandable button with padding

hSizer->Add(button2, 0, wxALL, 5); // Fixed-size button
with padding


wxBoxSizer*        vSizer        =        new
wxBoxSizer(wxVERTICAL);

vSizer->Add(hSizer, 0, wxALIGN_CENTER); // Center
the horizontal sizer

vSizer->Add(textCtrl, 1, wxEXPAND | wxALL, 5); //
Expandable text control
```

## 2. wxGridSizer

wxGridSizer arranges widgets in a grid with a fixed
number of rows and columns.

- **Creation:**

C++

```cpp
wxGridSizer* sizer = new wxGridSizer(rows, cols, vgap,
hgap);
```

- rows: Number of rows.
- cols: Number of columns.
- vgap: Vertical gap between widgets.
- hgap: Horizontal gap between widgets.
- **Adding widgets:**

C++

```
sizer->Add(widget, proportion, flags, border);
```

- Widgets are added to the grid row by row.
- **Example:**

C++

```
wxGridSizer* sizer = new wxGridSizer(2, 2, 5, 5); // 2x2 grid with 5px gaps

sizer->Add(button1, 0, wxEXPAND);

sizer->Add(button2, 0, wxEXPAND);

sizer->Add(textCtrl1, 1, wxEXPAND);

sizer->Add(textCtrl2, 1, wxEXPAND);
```

**3.** wxFlexGridSizer

wxFlexGridSizer is similar to wxGridSizer but allows for more flexibility. Rows and columns can have different sizes, and you can specify which rows or columns should grow if extra space is available.

- **Creation:** Same as wxGridSizer.
- **Adding widgets:** Same as wxGridSizer.
- **Flexibility:**

C++

```
sizer->AddGrowableRow(row); // Allow row to grow vertically

sizer->AddGrowableCol(col); // Allow column to grow horizontally
```

- **Example:**

C++

```
wxFlexGridSizer* sizer = new wxFlexGridSizer(2, 2, 5, 5);

sizer->Add(button, 0);

sizer->Add(textCtrl1, 1, wxEXPAND); // Expand textCtrl1 horizontally
```

```
sizer->AddGrowableCol(1); // Allow the second column
to grow

sizer->Add(textCtrl2, 1, wxEXPAND); // Expand
textCtrl2 vertically

sizer->AddGrowableRow(1); // Allow the second row to
grow
```

**Important Notes:**

- **Nesting sizers:** You can nest sizers within each other to create complex layouts.
- **Sizer ownership:** The parent window or panel takes ownership of the sizer, so you don't need to delete it explicitly.
- **Best practices:** Use sizers consistently for all your layouts to ensure your GUI adapts well to different window sizes and platforms.

By mastering these sizer types and their properties, you can achieve precise and flexible layout management in your wxWidgets applications, creating user interfaces that are both visually appealing and user-friendly.

# Common Mistakes: Incorrect sizer usage leading to layout issues

While sizers are powerful tools for layout management, using them incorrectly can lead to unexpected and frustrating results. Here are some common mistakes to avoid:

## 1. Forgetting to set the sizer

After creating a sizer and adding widgets to it, you must set it as the sizer for the parent window or panel. Otherwise, the sizer won't have any effect on the layout.

C++

```
// Incorrect: Sizer is not set for the panel

wxPanel* panel = new wxPanel(this, wxID_ANY);

wxBoxSizer* sizer = new wxBoxSizer(wxVERTICAL);

sizer->Add(button, 0, wxALL, 5);

// Missing: panel->SetSizer(sizer);
```

## 2. Incorrect proportions

Using incorrect proportions can lead to widgets not being sized or positioned as expected. Remember that proportions are relative to other widgets in the same sizer.

C++

```
// Incorrect: Both buttons will have fixed size

wxBoxSizer* sizer = new wxBoxSizer(wxHORIZONTAL);

sizer->Add(button1, 0, wxEXPAND); // Should have proportion 1 to expand

sizer->Add(button2, 0, wxEXPAND);
```

### 3. Overusing wxEXPAND

Using wxEXPAND for all widgets in a sizer can lead to unexpected behavior, especially in nested sizers. Use wxEXPAND judiciously only for widgets that should expand to fill available space.

C++

```
// Incorrect: Both sizers and the button will try to expand
```

```cpp
wxBoxSizer*        innerSizer        =        new
wxBoxSizer(wxHORIZONTAL);

innerSizer->Add(button, 0, wxEXPAND);


wxBoxSizer*        outerSizer        =        new
wxBoxSizer(wxVERTICAL);

outerSizer->Add(innerSizer, 0, wxEXPAND);
```

## 4. Not considering minimum size

Widgets have a minimum size that they need to display their content correctly. If you force a widget to be smaller than its minimum size, it might be truncated or not visible at all.

C++

```cpp
// Incorrect: Text control might be too small to display its label

wxTextCtrl*    textCtrl    =    new    wxTextCtrl(panel,
wxID_ANY, "Long Label");

sizer->Add(textCtrl, 0, wxALL, 5); // No size specified,
might be too small
```

## 5. Conflicting flags

Using conflicting flags can lead to undefined behavior. For example, wxALIGN_LEFT and wxALIGN_RIGHT cannot be used together.

C++

```
// Incorrect: Conflicting alignment flags

sizer->Add(button,    0,    wxALIGN_LEFT    |
wxALIGN_RIGHT);
```

## 6. Forgetting about borders and gaps

Borders and gaps in sizers affect the spacing between widgets. Not accounting for them can lead to widgets being too close or too far apart.

C++

```
// Incorrect: Buttons might be too close together

wxBoxSizer*    sizer    =    new
wxBoxSizer(wxHORIZONTAL);

sizer->Add(button1, 0, wxALL, 0); // No border
```

```
sizer->Add(button2, 0, wxALL, 0);
```

## 7. Not testing on different platforms

Layouts can look different on different platforms due to variations in widget sizes and styles. Always test your layouts on all target platforms to ensure they look and behave as expected.

### Best Practices

- **Plan your layout:** Before writing code, sketch out your desired layout and consider the different sizer types and their properties.
- **Start simple:** Begin with a basic sizer and gradually add complexity as needed.
- **Use** wxSizerFlags**:** wxSizerFlags provides a more convenient way to set proportions, flags, and borders.
- **Debug your layout:** If you encounter layout issues, use debugging tools to inspect the sizer hierarchy and widget properties.
- **Refer to the documentation:** The wxWidgets documentation provides detailed information on sizers and their usage.

By being mindful of these common mistakes and following best practices, you can avoid layout issues and create user interfaces that are visually appealing and user-friendly across different platforms.

## Best Practices: Using sizers effectively for responsive layouts

Creating responsive layouts in wxWidgets involves more than just throwing widgets into sizers. It requires a thoughtful approach to ensure your GUI adapts gracefully to different window sizes, screen resolutions, and platform variations. Here are some best practices to help you achieve truly responsive layouts:

### 1. Plan your layout

Before writing any code, sketch out your desired layout on paper or using a design tool. Think about the different screen sizes and orientations your application might be used on. Consider the relationships between widgets and how they should resize or reposition when the window size changes.

### 2. Choose the right sizer

Select the sizer type that best suits your layout needs.

- wxBoxSizer: Ideal for simple linear layouts (horizontal or vertical).

- wxGridSizer: Suitable for grid-like arrangements with a fixed number of rows and columns.
- wxFlexGridSizer: Provides more flexibility for grids with varying row and column sizes.
- wxStaticBoxSizer: Useful for grouping related controls within a labeled box.

### 3. Use proportions effectively

Proportions determine how much space a widget gets within a sizer. Use proportions of 0 for fixed-size widgets and 1 (or greater) for widgets that should expand to fill available space.

C++

```
sizer->Add(button, 0, wxALL, 5); // Fixed-size button

sizer->Add(textCtrl, 1, wxEXPAND | wxALL, 5); //
Expandable text control
```

### 4. Combine and nest sizers

Don't be afraid to combine different sizer types and nest them within each other to create complex layouts. This allows you to achieve hierarchical organization and fine-grained control over widget placement.

C++

```
wxBoxSizer*          innerSizer          =          new
wxBoxSizer(wxHORIZONTAL);

// ... add widgets to innerSizer ...


wxBoxSizer*          outerSizer          =          new
wxBoxSizer(wxVERTICAL);

outerSizer->Add(innerSizer, 0, wxALIGN_CENTER); //
Center the inner sizer

// ... add other widgets to outerSizer ...
```

## 5. Use wxSizerFlags

wxSizerFlags provides a more convenient and readable way to set proportions, flags, and borders for widgets added to a sizer.

C++

```
sizer->Add(button,
wxSizerFlags(0).Expand().Border(wxALL,     5));     //
Expandable button with padding
```

## 6. Handle minimum sizes

Be aware of the minimum size requirements of widgets. Don't force them to be smaller than their minimum size, as this can lead to truncation or clipping of content.

## 7. Test on different platforms

Different platforms may have variations in widget sizes and styles. Always test your layouts on all target platforms to ensure they look and behave as expected.

## 8. Use wxSplitterWindow

For layouts with resizable panes, consider using wxSplitterWindow. This allows users to interactively adjust the size of different sections of the window.

## 9. Consider wxAuiManager

For more advanced and dynamic layouts, explore wxAuiManager. This allows you to create dockable windows, toolbars, and perspectives, similar to what you find in many modern applications.

## 10. Keep it simple

While complex layouts are possible, strive for simplicity and clarity. Avoid overusing nested sizers or complex flag combinations, as this can make your code harder to maintain and debug.

By following these best practices, you can create responsive layouts in wxWidgets that adapt seamlessly to different window sizes and platforms, providing a consistent and user-friendly experience.

## Code samples: Creating complex layouts with nested sizers

C++

```cpp
#include <wx/wxprec.h>

#ifndef WX_PRECOMP

    #include <wx/wx.h>

#endif


class MyApp : public wxApp

{

public:

    virtual bool OnInit();

};
```

```cpp
class MyFrame : public wxFrame

{

public:

    MyFrame(const wxString& title, const
wxPoint& pos, const wxSize& size);

private:

    wxDECLARE_EVENT_TABLE();

};



wxBEGIN_EVENT_TABLE(MyFrame, wxFrame)

wxEND_EVENT_TABLE()



wxIMPLEMENT_APP(MyApp);



bool MyApp::OnInit()

{
```

```cpp
    MyFrame *frame = new MyFrame("Nested
Sizers",    wxPoint(50,    50),    wxSize(600,
400));

    frame->Show(true);

    return true;

}


MyFrame::MyFrame(const    wxString&    title,
const wxPoint& pos, const wxSize& size)

          : wxFrame(NULL, wxID_ANY, title,
pos, size)

{

    wxPanel* panel = new wxPanel(this,
wxID_ANY);



    // Create controls

    wxButton* button1 = new wxButton(panel,
wxID_ANY, "Button 1");

    wxButton* button2 = new wxButton(panel,
wxID_ANY, "Button 2");
```

```cpp
        wxTextCtrl*   textCtrl1   =   new
wxTextCtrl(panel, wxID_ANY, "");

        wxTextCtrl*   textCtrl2   =   new
wxTextCtrl(panel, wxID_ANY, "");

        wxStaticText*   label1   =   new
wxStaticText(panel, wxID_ANY, "Label 1:");

        .wxStaticText*   label2   =   new
wxStaticText(panel, wxID_ANY, "Label 2:");


    // Create nested sizers

        wxBoxSizer*   topSizer   =   new
wxBoxSizer(wxHORIZONTAL);



        wxBoxSizer*   leftSizer   =   new
wxBoxSizer(wxVERTICAL);

    leftSizer->Add(button1, 0, wxEXPAND |
wxALL, 5);

    leftSizer->Add(label1, 0, wxALL, 5);

    leftSizer->Add(textCtrl1, 1, wxEXPAND |
wxALL, 5); // Expand textCtrl1 vertically
```

```cpp
        wxBoxSizer* rightSizer = new
wxBoxSizer(wxVERTICAL);

    rightSizer->Add(button2, 0, wxEXPAND |
wxALL, 5);

    rightSizer->Add(label2, 0, wxALL, 5);

    rightSizer->Add(textCtrl2, 1, wxEXPAND
| wxALL, 5); // Expand textCtrl2 vertically


    topSizer->Add(leftSizer, 1, wxEXPAND |
wxALL,    10);    //    Expand    leftSizer
horizontally

    topSizer->Add(rightSizer, 1, wxEXPAND |
wxALL,    10);    //    Expand    rightSizer
horizontally


    // Set the top-level sizer for the
panel

    panel->SetSizer(topSizer);

}
```

## Explanation:

1. **Controls:** We create two buttons, two text controls, and two static text labels.
2. **Nested Sizers:**
   - topSizer: A horizontal wxBoxSizer to arrange the left and right sections of the layout.
   - leftSizer: A vertical wxBoxSizer to arrange the controls on the left side.
   - rightSizer: A vertical wxBoxSizer to arrange the controls on the right side.
3. **Adding Widgets:** Widgets are added to their respective sizers with appropriate proportions and flags.
4. **Setting the Sizer:** The topSizer is set as the sizer for the panel, which effectively applies the entire layout.

This example demonstrates how to use nested sizers to create a more complex layout. The topSizer divides the window horizontally, and the leftSizer and rightSizer arrange the controls within their respective sections. The use of wxEXPAND ensures that the text controls expand to fill the available space in their respective columns.

You can further expand this example by adding more controls, nesting sizers at multiple levels, and experimenting with different sizer types and flags to achieve the desired layout for your application.

# Practice: Designing a form with various controls and a well-organized layout

Let's put your sizer skills to the test by designing a user registration form. This exercise will challenge you to combine different controls and sizers to create a well-organized and visually appealing layout.

**Form Requirements:**

- **Fields:**
  - First Name (Text box)
  - Last Name (Text box)
  - Email (Text box)
  - Password (Password text box)
  - Confirm Password (Password text box)
  - Gender (Radio buttons: Male, Female, Other)
  - Country (Combo box with a list of countries)
  - Interests (Checkboxes: Reading, Sports, Music, Movies, Travel)
- **Buttons:**
  - Register
  - Cancel

**Layout Guidelines:**

- Use a wxGridSizer to arrange the labels and input fields in a grid-like format.
- Group related fields together (e.g., First Name and Last Name).
- Use a wxStaticBoxSizer to create a labeled box for the "Gender" options.
- Use a wxBoxSizer to arrange the "Interests" checkboxes horizontally.
- Place the "Register" and "Cancel" buttons at the bottom of the form, aligned to the right.
- Add appropriate spacing and borders to make the form look clean and organized.

**Example Structure (using wxSizerFlags for brevity):**

C++

```
// ... (In your frame or panel constructor) ...


wxPanel* panel = new wxPanel(this, wxID_ANY);


// Create controls

wxTextCtrl* firstNameText = new wxTextCtrl(panel, wxID_ANY, "");
```

// ... (Create other text controls, radio buttons, combo box, checkboxes) ...

```cpp
wxButton* registerButton = new wxButton(panel, wxID_ANY, "Register");

wxButton* cancelButton = new wxButton(panel, wxID_ANY, "Cancel");
```

// Create sizers

```cpp
wxGridSizer* gridSizer = new wxGridSizer(5, 2, 5, 5); // 5 rows, 2 columns, 5px gaps

wxStaticBoxSizer* genderSizer = new wxStaticBoxSizer(wxVERTICAL, panel, "Gender");

wxBoxSizer* interestsSizer = new wxBoxSizer(wxHORIZONTAL);

wxBoxSizer* buttonSizer = new wxBoxSizer(wxHORIZONTAL);

wxBoxSizer* mainSizer = new wxBoxSizer(wxVERTICAL);
```

// Add controls to gridSizer

```cpp
gridSizer->Add(new wxStaticText(panel, wxID_ANY,
"First Name:"), wxSizerFlags().AlignRight());

gridSizer->Add(firstNameText,
wxSizerFlags(1).Expand());

// ... (Add other labels and text controls to gridSizer) ...



// Add radio buttons to genderSizer

genderSizer->Add(maleRadio,
wxSizerFlags().Border(wxALL, 5));

// ... (Add other radio buttons to genderSizer) ...



// Add checkboxes to interestsSizer

interestsSizer->Add(readingCheck,
wxSizerFlags().Border(wxALL, 5));

// ... (Add other checkboxes to interestsSizer) ...



// Add buttons to buttonSizer
```

```
buttonSizer->Add(registerButton,
wxSizerFlags().Border(wxALL, 5));

buttonSizer->Add(cancelButton,
wxSizerFlags().Border(wxALL, 5));


// Add sizers to mainSizer

mainSizer->Add(gridSizer,
wxSizerFlags(1).Expand().Border(wxALL, 10));

mainSizer->Add(genderSizer,
wxSizerFlags().Expand().Border(wxALL, 10));

mainSizer->Add(new wxStaticText(panel, wxID_ANY,
"Interests:"),        wxSizerFlags().Border(wxLEFT       |
wxRIGHT | wxTOP, 10));

mainSizer->Add(interestsSizer,
wxSizerFlags().Expand().Border(wxLEFT | wxRIGHT |
wxBOTTOM, 10));

mainSizer->Add(buttonSizer,
wxSizerFlags().AlignRight().Border(wxALL, 10));


// Set the main sizer for the panel
```

```
panel->SetSizer(mainSizer);
```

This structure provides a starting point for your registration form. You can customize the controls, sizers, and layout further to match your specific design preferences and requirements. Remember to test your form on different platforms and window sizes to ensure it remains responsive and user-friendly.

# Chapter 6: Graphics and Drawing in wxWidgets

## Drawing Primitives: Lines, Rectangles, Circles

wxWidgets provides a powerful drawing API that allows you to create custom graphics and visualizations within your applications. This section focuses on the fundamental drawing primitives: lines, rectangles, and circles. You'll learn how to use the wxDC (Device Context) class to draw these shapes with various styles and colors.

### 1. The Device Context (wxDC)

The wxDC class is the core of wxWidgets' drawing API. It provides a common interface for drawing on different devices, such as the screen, a printer, or a bitmap. Think of it as a canvas on which you can paint various shapes and text.

- **Types of DCs:**
    - wxPaintDC: Used for drawing within a window's paint event handler.
    - wxClientDC: Used for drawing within a window's client area.
    - wxMemoryDC: Used for drawing on a bitmap in memory.

- wxPrinterDC: Used for drawing on a printer.

- **Obtaining a DC:**

C++

```
// In a window's paint event handler:

void MyWindow::OnPaint(wxPaintEvent& event) {

    wxPaintDC dc(this); // this refers to the window

    // ... draw on dc ...

}



// In other contexts:

wxClientDC dc(this); // Draw on the window's client area
```

## 2. Pens and Brushes

Before drawing shapes, you need to set the drawing tools:

- **Pen** (wxPen): Defines the style and color of lines and outlines.

- o wxPen(const wxColour& colour, int width = 1, wxPenStyle style = wxPENSTYLE_SOLID)
- **Brush (wxBrush):** Defines the color or pattern used to fill shapes.
  - o wxBrush(const wxColour& colour, wxBrushStyle style = wxBRUSHSTYLE_SOLID)
- **Setting pens and brushes:**

C++

```
wxPen redPen(wxColour(255, 0, 0), 3); // Red pen with width 3

dc.SetPen(redPen);



wxBrush blueBrush(wxColour(0, 0, 255)); // Solid blue brush

dc.SetBrush(blueBrush);
```

## 3. Drawing Lines

- DrawLine(wxCoord x1, wxCoord y1, wxCoord x2, wxCoord y2)

Draws a line from point (x1, y1) to point (x2, y2).

C++

dc.DrawLine(10, 10, 100, 50); // Draw a line from (10, 10) to (100, 50)

## 4. Drawing Rectangles

- DrawRectangle(wxCoord x, wxCoord y, wxCoord width, wxCoord height)

Draws a rectangle with the top-left corner at (x, y), the specified width and height.

C++

dc.DrawRectangle(20, 20, 80, 60); // Draw a rectangle at (20, 20) with width 80 and height 60

- DrawRoundedRectangle(wxCoord x, wxCoord y, wxCoord width, wxCoord height, double radius)

Draws a rectangle with rounded corners.

C++

dc.DrawRoundedRectangle(20, 20, 80, 60, 10); // Draw a rounded rectangle with a corner radius of 10

## 5. Drawing Circles and Ellipses

- DrawCircle(wxCoord x, wxCoord y, wxCoord radius)

Draws a circle with the center at (x, y) and the specified radius.

C++

dc.DrawCircle(100, 100, 50); // Draw a circle with center at (100, 100) and radius 50

- DrawEllipse(wxCoord x, wxCoord y, wxCoord width, wxCoord height)

Draws an ellipse within the specified bounding rectangle.

C++

dc.DrawEllipse(20, 100, 80, 60); // Draw an ellipse within the rectangle at (20, 100) with width 80 and height 60

## 6. Other Drawing Functions

wxDC provides many other drawing functions, including:

- DrawPoint(wxCoord x, wxCoord y): Draws a single point.
- DrawLines(int n, const wxPoint points[], wxCoord xoffset = 0, wxCoord yoffset = 0): Draws multiple connected lines.
- DrawPolygon(int n, const wxPoint points[], wxCoord xoffset = 0, wxCoord yoffset = 0, wxPolygonFillMode fillStyle = wxODDEVEN_RULE): Draws a polygon.
- DrawText(const wxString& text, wxCoord x, wxCoord y): Draws text.

**Example:**

C++

```
void MyPanel::OnPaint(wxPaintEvent& event) {

    wxPaintDC dc(this);


    dc.SetPen(*wxBLACK_PEN); // Use the default black
pen
```

```
    dc.SetBrush(*wxRED_BRUSH); // Use the default
red brush


    dc.DrawLine(10, 10, 100, 100);

    dc.DrawRectangle(120, 10, 80, 60);

    dc.DrawRoundedRectangle(220, 10, 80, 60, 10);

    dc.DrawCircle(350, 50, 40);

    dc.DrawEllipse(10, 120, 80, 60);

}
```

This example demonstrates how to draw basic shapes using wxDC. You can combine these primitives and explore other drawing functions to create more complex graphics and visualizations in your wxWidgets applications.

## Working with Colors and Fonts

Colors and fonts play a crucial role in the visual appeal and readability of your wxWidgets applications. They can enhance the user experience, convey information effectively, and reinforce your application's branding.

This section explores how to work with colors and fonts in wxWidgets.

**1. Colors** (wxColour)

The wxColour class represents colors in wxWidgets. You can create colors using various constructors:

- **RGB values:**

C++

```
wxColour red(255, 0, 0); // Red

wxColour green(0, 255, 0); // Green

wxColour blue(0, 0, 255); // Blue
```

- **Hexadecimal values:**

C++

```
wxColour orange("#FFA500"); // Orange
```

- **Color names:**

C++

wxColour cyan(wxT("CYAN")); // Cyan

- **Predefined colors:**

C++

wxColour white(*wxWHITE); // White

wxColour black(*wxBLACK); // Black

- **Key methods:**
  - GetRed(), GetGreen(), GetBlue(): Get the RGB components of the color.
  - Set(unsigned char red, unsigned char green, unsigned char blue): Set the RGB components.
  - IsOk(): Check if the color is valid.

## 2. Setting Colors in wxDC

You can set colors for drawing using the SetPen() and SetBrush() methods of wxDC:

C++

wxPaintDC dc(this);

wxColour myColor(100, 150, 200);

wxPen myPen(myColor, 2); // Pen with the specified color and width

dc.SetPen(myPen);

wxBrush myBrush(myColor); // Solid brush with the specified color

dc.SetBrush(myBrush);

dc.DrawRectangle(10, 10, 100, 80); // Draw a rectangle with the set pen and brush

## 3. Fonts (wxFont)

The wxFont class represents fonts in wxWidgets. You can create fonts using the following constructor:

C++

wxFont(int pointSize, wxFontFamily family, wxFontStyle style, wxFontWeight weight, bool underline = false, const wxString& faceName = wxEmptyString,

wxFontEncoding encoding = wxFONTENCODING_DEFAULT)

- **Parameters:**
    - pointSize: The font size in points.
    - family: The font family (e.g., wxFONTFAMILY_DEFAULT, wxFONTFAMILY_ROMAN, wxFONTFAMILY_SWISS).
    - style: The font style (e.g., wxFONTSTYLE_NORMAL, wxFONTSTYLE_ITALIC, wxFONTSTYLE_SLANT).
    - weight: The font weight (e.g., wxFONTWEIGHT_NORMAL, wxFONTWEIGHT_BOLD, wxFONTWEIGHT_LIGHT).
    - underline: Whether the font should be underlined.
    - faceName: The name of the font face (e.g., "Arial", "Times New Roman").
    - encoding: The font encoding.
- **Example:**

C++

```
wxFont myFont(12, wxFONTFAMILY_SWISS,
wxFONTSTYLE_NORMAL,
wxFONTWEIGHT_BOLD);
```

## 4. Setting Fonts in wxDC

You can set the font for drawing text using the SetFont()
method of wxDC:

C++

```
wxPaintDC dc(this);
```

```
wxFont myFont(14, wxFONTFAMILY_ROMAN,
wxFONTSTYLE_ITALIC,
wxFONTWEIGHT_NORMAL);
```

```
dc.SetFont(myFont);
```

```
dc.DrawText("Hello, wxWidgets!", 10, 10); // Draw text
with the set font
```

## 5. Font Dialog (wxFontDialog)

The wxFontDialog class provides a dialog box that allows the user to select a font. You can use it to let users customize the font in your application.

C++

```
wxFontData data;

wxFontDialog dialog(this, data);

if (dialog.ShowModal() == wxID_OK) {

    wxFontData retData = dialog.GetFontData();

    wxFont font = retData.GetChosenFont();

    // ... use the selected font ...

}
```

## 6. System Colors and Fonts

wxWidgets provides access to system colors and fonts, allowing your application to blend in with the user's operating system theme.

- **System colors:** wxSystemSettings::GetColour(wxSystemColour index)

- **System                                     fonts:**
  wxSystemSettings::GetFont(wxSystemFont
  index)

By effectively using colors and fonts, you can create
visually appealing and user-friendly wxWidgets
applications. Experiment with different combinations to
find what works best for your application's design and
purpose.

## Handling Images and Bitmaps

Images are essential for creating visually rich and
engaging user interfaces. wxWidgets provides
comprehensive support for loading, displaying, and
manipulating images and bitmaps. This section explores
how to work with images in your wxWidgets
applications.

**1. Image Classes**

wxWidgets offers two main classes for handling images:

- wxImage: Represents an image in memory. It
  provides functions for loading images from
  various file formats (e.g., PNG, JPEG, GIF,
  BMP), accessing pixel data, converting between
  formats, and more.
- wxBitmap: Represents a platform-specific
  bitmap that can be drawn on a wxDC. It's often

created from a wxImage and is used for displaying images on screen.

## 2. Loading Images

You can load images from files using the wxImage class:

C++

```
wxImage image;

if                    (image.LoadFile("my_image.png",
wxBITMAP_TYPE_PNG)) {

   // Image loaded successfully

} else {

   // Error loading image

}
```

- LoadFile() takes the file name and the image type as arguments.
- You can use wxBITMAP_TYPE_ANY to let wxWidgets auto-detect the image type.

## 3. Creating Bitmaps

Once you have a wxImage, you can create a wxBitmap from it:

C++

wxBitmap bitmap(image);

## 4. Displaying Images

To display an image on screen, you draw the wxBitmap on a wxDC:

C++

```
void MyPanel::OnPaint(wxPaintEvent& event) {
    wxPaintDC dc(this);


    // ... load and create bitmap (as shown above) ...


    dc.DrawBitmap(bitmap, 10, 10, true); // Draw the bitmap at (10, 10)
}
```

## 5. Scaling and Resizing

You can scale or resize images using the Rescale() and Resize() methods of wxImage:

C++

```
wxImage scaledImage = image.Scale(newWidth,
newHeight, wxIMAGE_QUALITY_HIGH);

wxBitmap scaledBitmap(scaledImage);
```

```
wxImage resizedImage = image.Resize(newSize,
wxPoint(0, 0), red, green, blue);

wxBitmap resizedBitmap(resizedImage);
```

- Rescale() scales the image to the specified dimensions while maintaining the aspect ratio.
- Resize() resizes the image to the specified dimensions, optionally filling any extra space with a background color.

## 6. Manipulating Images

wxImage provides various functions for manipulating images:

- Rotate(): Rotates the image.
- Mirror(): Mirrors the image horizontally or vertically.
- ConvertToGreyscale(): Converts the image to greyscale.
- GetSubImage(const wxRect& rect): Extracts a sub-image.

## 7. Saving Images

You can save images to files using the SaveFile() method of wxImage:

C++

```
if            (image.SaveFile("modified_image.jpg",
wxBITMAP_TYPE_JPEG)) {

    // Image saved successfully

} else {

    // Error saving image

}
```

## 8. Using Stock Images

wxWidgets provides a set of stock images for common icons and symbols:

C++

```
wxBitmap stockBitmap =
wxArtProvider::GetBitmap(wxART_INFORMATION,
wxART_OTHER, wxSize(32, 32));
```

- wxART_INFORMATION, wxART_WARNING, wxART_ERROR, etc. are predefined art IDs.

By mastering these image handling techniques, you can enhance the visual appeal and functionality of your wxWidgets applications. You can load, display, manipulate, and save images to create engaging and informative user interfaces.

## Code samples: Creating a simple drawing application

C++

```
#include <wx/wxprec.h>

#ifndef WX_PRECOMP

    #include <wx/wx.h>
```

```cpp
#endif


class MyApp : public wxApp
{
public:
    virtual bool OnInit();
};


class MyFrame : public wxFrame
{
public:
        MyFrame(const wxString& title, const
wxPoint& pos, const wxSize& size);


private:
    void OnPaint(wxPaintEvent& event);

    void OnMouseDown(wxMouseEvent& event);

    void OnMouseMove(wxMouseEvent& event);
```

```cpp
    void OnMouseUp(wxMouseEvent& event);

    void OnClear(wxCommandEvent& event);


    wxPanel* drawingPanel;

    bool isDrawing;

    wxPoint lastPoint;


    wxDECLARE_EVENT_TABLE();
};


wxBEGIN_EVENT_TABLE(MyFrame, wxFrame)

    EVT_PAINT(MyFrame::OnPaint)

    EVT_LEFT_DOWN(MyFrame::OnMouseDown)

    EVT_MOTION(MyFrame::OnMouseMove)

    EVT_LEFT_UP(MyFrame::OnMouseUp)

    EVT_BUTTON(wxID_ANY, MyFrame::OnClear)
// Assuming a "Clear" button exists

wxEND_EVENT_TABLE()
```

```cpp
wxIMPLEMENT_APP(MyApp);


bool MyApp::OnInit()

{

    MyFrame *frame = new MyFrame("Simple
Drawing App", wxPoint(50, 50), wxSize(800,
600));

    frame->Show(true);

    return true;

}



MyFrame::MyFrame(const   wxString&   title,
const wxPoint& pos, const wxSize& size)

        : wxFrame(NULL, wxID_ANY, title,
pos, size)

{

    drawingPanel = new wxPanel(this,
wxID_ANY);

    isDrawing = false;
```

```cpp
    // Create a "Clear" button (you'll need
to add it to a sizer)

        wxButton*  clearButton  =  new
wxButton(this, wxID_ANY, "Clear");

}



void  MyFrame::OnPaint(wxPaintEvent&  event)
{

    wxPaintDC  dc(drawingPanel);  //  Use
wxPaintDC with the panel

    // ... any additional drawing code can
go here ...

}



void     MyFrame::OnMouseDown(wxMouseEvent&
event) {

    isDrawing = true;

    lastPoint = event.GetPosition();

}
```

```cpp
void      MyFrame::OnMouseMove(wxMouseEvent&
event) {

    if (isDrawing) {

        wxClientDC dc(drawingPanel); // Use
wxClientDC for drawing outside of OnPaint

        dc.SetPen(*wxBLACK_PEN);

                    dc.DrawLine(lastPoint,
event.GetPosition());

        lastPoint = event.GetPosition();

    }

}



void      MyFrame::OnMouseUp(wxMouseEvent&
event) {

    isDrawing = false;

}



void      MyFrame::OnClear(wxCommandEvent&
event) {
```

```
    drawingPanel->Refresh(); ` // Clear the
panel by triggering a repaint event

}
```

## Explanation:

1. MyFrame **Class:**
   - drawingPanel: A wxPanel where the drawing will take place.
   - isDrawing: A boolean to track if the mouse button is currently pressed.
   - lastPoint: Stores the previous mouse position for drawing lines.

2. **Event Handlers:**
   - OnPaint: Currently empty, but you can add code here to draw static elements or a background.
   - OnMouseDown: Sets isDrawing to true and stores the initial mouse position.
   - OnMouseMove: If isDrawing is true, draws a line from the last point to the current mouse position using wxClientDC.
   - OnMouseUp: Sets isDrawing to false to stop drawing.

o OnClear: Clears the drawing panel by calling Refresh(), which triggers a repaint event.

3. **Important Notes:**

o wxClientDC **vs.** wxPaintDC: wxPaintDC is used within the OnPaint handler, while wxClientDC is used for drawing outside of OnPaint, such as in response to mouse events.

o **Drawing on the Panel:** Make sure you are drawing on the drawingPanel and not directly on the frame.

o **Clearing the Panel:** The OnClear handler clears the panel by refreshing it, causing the OnPaint handler to be called again.

This example provides a basic framework for a simple drawing application. You can extend it further by adding features like:

- Different colors and pen styles.
- Drawing shapes other than lines (e.g., rectangles, circles).
- An eraser tool.
- Saving and loading drawings.

Practice: Implementing a basic image viewer

C++

```cpp
#include <wx/wxprec.h>

#ifndef WX_PRECOMP
    #include <wx/wx.h>
#endif


#include <wx/filedlg.h> // For the file
dialog


class MyApp : public wxApp
{
public:
    virtual bool OnInit();
};


class MyFrame : public wxFrame
{
public:
    MyFrame(const wxString& title, const
wxPoint& pos, const wxSize& size);
```

```cpp
private:

    void OnOpen(wxCommandEvent& event);

    void OnPaint(wxPaintEvent& event);


    wxImage image;

    wxBitmap bitmap;

    wxPanel* imagePanel; // Panel to hold
the image


    wxDECLARE_EVENT_TABLE();
};


enum

{

    ID_Open = 1,

};
```

```cpp
wxBEGIN_EVENT_TABLE(MyFrame, wxFrame)

    EVT_MENU(ID_Open, MyFrame::OnOpen)

    EVT_PAINT(MyFrame::OnPaint)

wxEND_EVENT_TABLE()


wxIMPLEMENT_APP(MyApp);


bool MyApp::OnInit()

{

    MyFrame *frame = new MyFrame("Image
Viewer", wxPoint(50, 50), wxSize(800,
600));

    frame->Show(true);

    return true;

}


MyFrame::MyFrame(const wxString& title,
const wxPoint& pos, const wxSize& size)
```

```cpp
                 : wxFrame(NULL, wxID_ANY, title,
pos, size)
{
    // Create menu bar

    wxMenu *menuFile = new wxMenu;

                menuFile->Append(ID_Open,
"&Open\tCtrl-O");



    wxMenuBar *menuBar = new wxMenuBar;

    menuBar->Append(menuFile, "&File");

    SetMenuBar(menuBar);


    // Create image panel

        imagePanel  =  new  wxPanel(this,
wxID_ANY);
}



void MyFrame::OnOpen(wxCommandEvent& event)
{
```

```cpp
    wxFileDialog openFileDialog(this,
_("Open Image"), "", "",

                        "Image files
(*.jpg;*.png;*.bmp)|*.jpg;*.png;*.bmp",
wxFD_OPEN | wxFD_FILE_MUST_EXIST);

    if (openFileDialog.ShowModal() ==
wxID_CANCEL)

    return;




                        if
(image.LoadFile(openFileDialog.GetPath()))
{

    bitmap = wxBitmap(image);

    imagePanel->Refresh(); // Trigger a
repaint to display the image

    } else {

        wxLogError("Cannot open file
'%s'.", openFileDialog.GetPath());

    }

}
```

```
void MyFrame::OnPaint(wxPaintEvent& event)
{

    wxPaintDC dc(imagePanel);  // Use
wxPaintDC with the panel

    if (bitmap.IsOk()) {

        dc.DrawBitmap(bitmap, 0, 0, true);

    }

}
```

**Explanation:**

1. MyFrame **Class:**
   - image: A wxImage object to store the loaded image.
   - bitmap: A wxBitmap object created from the wxImage for drawing.
   - imagePanel: A wxPanel to hold and display the image.
2. OnOpen **Handler:**
   - Opens a file dialog to select an image file.
   - Loads the selected image file into the image object.
   - Creates a wxBitmap from the loaded image.

- Calls Refresh() on the imagePanel to trigger a repaint and display the image.
3. OnPaint **Handler:**
   - Gets a wxPaintDC for the imagePanel.
   - If the bitmap is valid (i.e., an image has been loaded), it draws the bitmap on the panel using DrawBitmap().

**Key Improvements:**

- **Image Panel:** The image is now drawn on a dedicated panel (imagePanel) instead of directly on the frame. This allows for better control over the image display and avoids potential issues with redrawing other frame elements.
- **Error Handling:** The OnOpen handler checks if the image file was loaded successfully and displays an error message if not.
- **File Dialog:** The file dialog now filters for common image file types (JPG, PNG, BMP).

This basic image viewer provides a foundation for building more advanced image-related applications. You can extend it further by adding features like:

- **Zooming and panning:** Allow the user to zoom in and out of the image and pan around.
- **Image manipulation:** Implement basic image editing features like rotating, resizing, or applying filters.

- **Thumbnail view:** Display thumbnails of multiple images.
- **Slideshow mode:** Automatically display a sequence of images.

# Chapter 7: Advanced wxWidgets Topics

## Custom Widget Creation

While wxWidgets provides a rich set of built-in widgets, you might encounter situations where you need a unique visual element or specialized functionality not offered by the standard controls. In such cases, wxWidgets allows you to create your own custom widgets. This section explores the process of creating custom widgets, empowering you to extend wxWidgets' capabilities and tailor your applications to specific needs.

### 1. Why Create Custom Widgets?

- **Unique Visuals:** Design GUI elements with a distinct look and feel that aligns with your application's branding or visual style.
- **Specialized Functionality:** Implement behavior not found in standard widgets, such as custom data visualizations, interactive elements, or specialized input controls.
- **Code Reusability:** Encapsulate complex UI logic into reusable components, improving code organization and maintainability.

### 2. Approaches to Custom Widget Creation

wxWidgets offers two main approaches to creating custom widgets:

- **Generic Widgets:** Built on top of existing wxWidgets classes (wxControl or wxWindow). These widgets are rendered using wxWidgets' own drawing mechanisms, ensuring consistency across platforms but potentially sacrificing a native look and feel.
- **Native Widgets:** Directly utilize the underlying native toolkit widgets of each platform (e.g., GTK+ on Linux, Win32 on Windows, Cocoa on macOS). This provides a native look and feel but requires platform-specific implementations.

### 3. Creating a Generic Widget

Here's a basic structure for creating a generic custom widget derived from wxControl:

C++

```cpp
#include <wx/wx.h>


class MyCustomWidget : public wxControl
{
public:
```

```cpp
    MyCustomWidget(wxWindow* parent, wxWindowID id,
            const wxPoint& pos = wxDefaultPosition,
            const wxSize& size = wxDefaultSize,
            long style = 0);


    // ... other constructors, methods, and event handlers ...


protected:
    void OnPaint(wxPaintEvent& event) override; // Handle painting the widget
    void OnSize(wxSizeEvent& event) override; // Handle resizing
    void OnMouseClick(wxMouseEvent& event); // Handle mouse clicks
    // ... other event handlers ...


private:
    // ... data members to store widget state ...
```

```
    wxDECLARE_EVENT_TABLE();

};
```

- **Derivation:** Inherit from wxControl or wxWindow depending on the desired level of functionality.
- **Constructor:** Initialize the widget, setting its properties and creating any child windows or controls.
- **Event Handling:** Override event handlers like OnPaint, OnSize, OnMouseClick, etc., to respond to user interactions and update the widget's appearance.
- **Drawing:** Use wxDC within the OnPaint handler to draw the widget's visual representation.

## 4. Creating a Native Widget

Creating a native widget involves using platform-specific APIs and toolkits. This requires a deeper understanding of the native windowing systems and potentially writing separate code for each platform you want to support.

## 5. Key Considerations

- **Window Sizing:** Handle size events to ensure the widget resizes correctly and its contents are laid out appropriately.
- **Event Handling:** Implement custom events to notify other parts of your application about changes in the widget's state.
- **Accessibility:** Consider accessibility features to make your widget usable by people with disabilities.
- **Documentation:** Provide clear documentation for your custom widget, including its usage, properties, and events.

## 6. Example: A Simple Progress Bar

C++

```cpp
#include <wx/wx.h>


class MyProgressBar : public wxControl
{
public:
    MyProgressBar(wxWindow* parent, wxWindowID id,
                  const wxPoint& pos = wxDefaultPosition,
                  const wxSize& size = wxDefaultSize,
```

```cpp
                    long style = 0)
        : wxControl(parent, id, pos, size, style)
        , m_progress(0) {}

    void SetProgress(int progress) {
        m_progress = progress;
        Refresh();
    }

protected:
    void OnPaint(wxPaintEvent& event) override;

private:
    int m_progress;

    wxDECLARE_EVENT_TABLE();
};
```

```cpp
wxBEGIN_EVENT_TABLE(MyProgressBar,
wxControl)

    EVT_PAINT(MyProgressBar::OnPaint)

wxEND_EVENT_TABLE()


void MyProgressBar::OnPaint(wxPaintEvent& event) {
    wxPaintDC dc(this);
    wxRect rect = GetClientRect();


    dc.SetPen(*wxBLACK_PEN);
    dc.SetBrush(*wxGREEN_BRUSH);


    int width = (rect.width * m_progress) / 100;
    dc.DrawRectangle(0, 0, width, rect.height);
}
```

This example demonstrates a simple progress bar widget
that draws a filled rectangle representing the progress

value. You can use this as a starting point for creating more complex and visually appealing custom widgets.

By creating custom widgets, you can enhance the functionality and uniqueness of your wxWidgets applications. This allows you to build truly custom user interfaces tailored to your specific needs and design preferences.

## Event Handling and Filtering

Event handling is the core of interactive GUI applications. In wxWidgets, you can handle events using event tables (as discussed in Chapter 3) or by binding event handlers dynamically. This section explores advanced event handling techniques, including event filtering and dynamic event binding.

### 1. Event Tables Revisited

Event tables provide a static and efficient way to connect events with their corresponding handler functions. They are defined using macros like EVT_BUTTON, EVT_TEXT, EVT_MOTION, etc.

C++

```
wxBEGIN_EVENT_TABLE(MyFrame, wxFrame)
    EVT_BUTTON(wxID_OK, MyFrame::OnOK)
```

```
    EVT_CLOSE(MyFrame::OnClose)

wxEND_EVENT_TABLE()
```

- **Pros:**
  - Simple and easy to understand.
  - Efficient compile-time binding.
  - Good for organizing event handlers within a class.
- **Cons:**
  - Less flexible than dynamic binding.
  - Not suitable for situations where connections need to be changed at runtime.

## 2. Dynamic Event Binding with Bind()

The Bind() method provides a more flexible way to connect events with handlers at runtime. You can use it to bind events to any callable object, including member functions, static functions, and lambda expressions.

C++

```
button->Bind(wxEVT_BUTTON,
&MyFrame::OnButtonClicked, this); // Bind to a
member function
```

C++

```cpp
button->Bind(wxEVT_BUTTON,
[](wxCommandEvent& event){

    // ... handle the button click ...

}); // Bind to a lambda expression
```

- **Pros:**
    - More flexible than event tables.
    - Allows connecting events to any callable object.
    - Supports connecting and disconnecting events at runtime.
- **Cons:**
    - Can be less efficient than event tables due to runtime overhead.

### 3. Event Filtering

Event filtering allows you to intercept and process events before they reach their intended target. This can be useful for:

- **Modifying event behavior:** Change event properties or prevent them from being processed further.
- **Implementing custom logic:** Perform actions based on events before they reach the target widget.
- **Debugging:** Inspect events to understand the flow of events in your application.

## 4. Implementing an Event Filter

To implement an event filter, you need to:

- **Create a class derived from** wxEvtHandler**:** This class will contain your event filtering logic.
- **Override the** ProcessEvent() **method:** This method is called for each event that the filter is registered to handle.
- **Register the filter with a window:** Use the PushEventHandler() or AddEventHandler() method of the window to register the filter.

C++

```
class MyEventFilter : public wxEvtHandler
{
public:
    bool ProcessEvent(wxEvent& event) override {
```

```cpp
        if (event.GetEventType() ==
wxEVT_KEY_DOWN) {

            wxKeyEvent& keyEvent =
static_cast<wxKeyEvent&>(event);

        if (keyEvent.GetKeyCode() == WXK_ESCAPE)
{

            // ... handle Escape key press ...

            return true; // Prevent further processing of the
event

        }

    }

    return wxEvtHandler::ProcessEvent(event); // Pass
the event to the next handler

    }

};


// In your frame or window:

MyEventFilter* filter = new MyEventFilter();

this->PushEventHandler(filter); // Register the filter
```

## 5. Filtering Events at the Application Level

You can filter events at the application level by installing an event filter on the wxApp object. This allows you to intercept events for all windows in your application.

C++

```
// In your MyApp::OnInit() function:
MyEventFilter* filter = new MyEventFilter();
this->PushEventHandler(filter);
```

## 6. Removing an Event Filter

To remove an event filter, use the RemoveEventHandler() or PopEventHandler() method of the window.

C++

```
this->RemoveEventHandler(filter);
```

By understanding and utilizing these advanced event handling techniques, you can gain fine-grained control over the behavior of your wxWidgets applications. Event filtering and dynamic binding provide powerful tools for creating responsive and interactive user interfaces.

## Multithreading in wxWidgets

Modern applications often need to perform tasks in the background without blocking the user interface. This is where multithreading comes in. Multithreading allows you to execute multiple threads of execution concurrently, improving responsiveness and performance. wxWidgets provides a framework for creating and managing threads in your GUI applications.

### 1. Why Use Multithreading?

- **Responsiveness:** Prevent long-running operations from freezing the UI.
- **Performance:** Utilize multiple CPU cores for parallel processing.
- **Background Tasks:** Perform tasks like network communication, file I/O, or complex calculations in the background.

### 2. wxWidgets Threading Classes

- wxThread: The base class for creating threads.
- wxMutex: Used for synchronizing access to shared resources between threads.
- wxCriticalSection: Similar to wxMutex, but more efficient for single-process applications.

- **wxCondition:** Allows threads to wait for specific conditions.
- **wxThreadEvent:** Used for communication between threads.

## 3. Creating a Thread

To create a thread, you need to:

- **Derive a class from** wxThread**:** This class will contain the code that runs in the new thread.
- **Override the** Entry() **method:** This method is the entry point for the thread's execution.
- **Create an instance of your thread class and call** Create()**:** This creates the thread object.
- **Call** Run() **to start the thread:** This starts the thread's execution.

C++

```cpp
class MyThread : public wxThread
{
public:
    MyThread() : wxThread(wxTHREAD_DETACHED)
{} // Detached thread


    virtual ExitCode Entry() override {
```

```
// ... perform long-running task here ...

    return (ExitCode)0; // Return a value to indicate
success or failure

  }

};
```

```
// In your frame or window:

MyThread* thread = new MyThread();

if (thread->Create() != wxTHREAD_NO_ERROR) {

  // Handle thread creation error

}

thread->Run();
```

## 4. Thread Safety and Synchronization

When multiple threads access shared data, you need to
ensure thread safety to prevent data corruption.
wxWidgets provides synchronization objects like
wxMutex and wxCriticalSection to protect shared
resources.

```C++
wxMutex myMutex;

void MyFunction() {
    wxMutexLocker lock(myMutex); // Acquire the
mutex lock

    // ... access shared data ...
} // Mutex is automatically released when lock goes out
of scope
```

## 5. Communicating with the Main Thread

It's generally not safe to directly access GUI elements from a secondary thread. Instead, you should use wxThreadEvent to communicate with the main thread and update the UI.

```C++
// In your thread's Entry() method:
wxThreadEvent*          event          =          new
wxThreadEvent(wxEVT_THREAD, MY_EVENT_ID);
```

```
event->SetInt(result); // Set event data

wxQueueEvent(this, event); // Send the event to the main
thread


// In your frame or window's event table:

EVT_THREAD(MY_EVENT_ID,
MyFrame::OnThreadEvent)


void        MyFrame::OnThreadEvent(wxThreadEvent&
event) {

   int result = event.GetInt();

   // ... update UI based on result ...

}
```

## 6. wxWidgets and std::thread

While wxWidgets provides its own threading classes,
you can also use std::thread from the C++ standard
library in your wxWidgets applications. However, you
need to be careful about thread safety and
communication with the main thread when using
std::thread.

## 7. Best Practices

- **Minimize shared data:** Reduce the need for synchronization by minimizing the amount of data shared between threads.
- **Keep the GUI thread responsive:** Avoid performing long-running operations on the GUI thread.
- **Use thread-safe methods:** When accessing wxWidgets objects from secondary threads, use thread-safe methods like wxQueueEvent.
- **Handle thread termination:** Ensure proper cleanup and resource release when threads terminate.

By understanding and applying these multithreading concepts, you can create responsive and efficient wxWidgets applications that perform tasks in the background without affecting the user experience.

## Cross-Platform Considerations

One of the primary advantages of using wxWidgets is its ability to create cross-platform GUI applications. However, achieving true cross-platform compatibility requires careful consideration of various factors. This section explores key aspects of cross-platform development with wxWidgets, helping you build applications that look and feel native on different operating systems.

**1. Platform-Specific Code**

While wxWidgets abstracts away many platform differences, there might be situations where you need to write platform-specific code to access certain features or handle platform-specific behaviors.

- **Conditional Compilation:** Use preprocessor directives (#ifdef, #elif, #endif) to include or exclude code based on the target platform.

C++

```
#ifdef __WXMSW__
    // Windows-specific code
#elif __WXGTK__
    // Linux (GTK+) specific code
#elif __WXMAC__
    // macOS-specific code
#endif
```

- **Platform-Specific APIs:** In some cases, you might need to directly call platform-specific APIs to access functionalities not exposed by wxWidgets.

## 2. Look and Feel

wxWidgets strives to provide a native look and feel by using the native widgets of each platform whenever possible. However, there might be subtle differences in appearance and behavior across platforms.

- **Widget Styles:** Be aware that the appearance and behavior of certain widgets might vary slightly across platforms.
- **Layout Adjustments:** Fine-tune your layouts to account for differences in font sizes, widget spacing, and default window sizes on different platforms.
- **Testing:** Thoroughly test your application on all target platforms to ensure a consistent look and feel.

## 3. File System Differences

File paths and directory structures can differ significantly between operating systems. Use wxWidgets' file system classes (wxFileName, wxDir) to handle file paths in a platform-independent way.

- **Path Separators:** Use wxFileName::GetPathSeparator() to get the correct path separator for the current platform.
- **Home Directory:** Use wxStandardPaths::Get().GetUserHomeDir() to get the user's home directory.

## 4. Line Endings

Different operating systems use different line ending conventions (Windows: CRLF, Linux/macOS: LF). When reading or writing text files, use wxTextFile or handle line endings explicitly to ensure consistency.

## 5. Keyboard Shortcuts

Keyboard shortcuts can vary across platforms (e.g., Ctrl+C vs. Cmd+C). Provide platform-specific shortcuts or use generic shortcuts that work on all platforms.

## 6. Internationalization

If your application needs to support multiple languages, use wxWidgets' internationalization features (wxLocale, wxGetTranslation()) to handle translations and locale-specific settings.

## 7. Packaging and Deployment

Packaging and deploying your application on different platforms can be challenging. Use platform-specific tools and techniques to create installers or packages for each target platform.

## 8. Testing and Debugging

Thoroughly test your application on all target platforms to identify and fix any platform-specific issues. Use debugging tools and techniques to diagnose problems in different environments.

**Best Practices**

- **Use wxWidgets' cross-platform APIs:** Whenever possible, use wxWidgets' built-in functions and classes to handle platform-specific tasks.
- **Minimize platform-specific code:** Keep platform-specific code to a minimum to improve maintainability and reduce the risk of platform-specific bugs.
- **Test early and often:** Test your application on different platforms throughout the development process to catch compatibility issues early on.
- **Use a consistent coding style:** Maintain a consistent coding style across your project to improve readability and maintainability.

By following these guidelines and best practices, you can effectively address cross-platform considerations and build wxWidgets applications that work seamlessly on different operating systems, providing a consistent and native user experience.

## Real-world usage examples: Building a cross-platform file explorer

C++

```cpp
#include <wx/wxprec.h>

#ifndef WX_PRECOMP

    #include <wx/wx.h>

#endif


#include <wx/treectrl.h>

#include <wx/listctrl.h>

#include <wx/dir.h>

#include <wx/filename.h>


class MyApp : public wxApp
```

```cpp
{
public:
    virtual bool OnInit();
};


class MyFrame : public wxFrame
{
public:
    MyFrame(const wxString& title, const
wxPoint& pos, const wxSize& size);


private:
    void OnTreeItemActivated(wxTreeEvent&
event);

    void OnListItemActivated(wxListEvent&
event);

    void PopulateTree(wxTreeCtrl* treeCtrl,
const wxString& path, wxTreeItemId parent);

    void PopulateList(wxListCtrl* listCtrl,
const wxString& path);
```

```cpp
    wxTreeCtrl* treeCtrl;

    wxListCtrl* listCtrl;


    wxDECLARE_EVENT_TABLE();
};


wxBEGIN_EVENT_TABLE(MyFrame, wxFrame)

        EVT_TREE_ITEM_ACTIVATED(wxID_ANY,
MyFrame::OnTreeItemActivated)

        EVT_LIST_ITEM_ACTIVATED(wxID_ANY,
MyFrame::OnListItemActivated)

wxEND_EVENT_TABLE()


wxIMPLEMENT_APP(MyApp);


bool MyApp::OnInit()
{
```

```cpp
    MyFrame *frame = new MyFrame("File
Explorer", wxPoint(50, 50), wxSize(800,
600));

    frame->Show(true);

    return true;

}


MyFrame::MyFrame(const wxString& title,
const wxPoint& pos, const wxSize& size)

            : wxFrame(NULL, wxID_ANY, title,
pos, size)

{

        wxSplitterWindow* splitter = new
wxSplitterWindow(this, wxID_ANY);


    // Create tree control

    treeCtrl = new wxTreeCtrl(splitter,
wxID_ANY, wxDefaultPosition, wxDefaultSize,
wxTR_DEFAULT_STYLE);

                wxTreeItemId rootId =
treeCtrl->AddRoot("/");
```

```cpp
    PopulateTree(treeCtrl, "/", rootId);


    // Create list control
    listCtrl = new wxListCtrl(splitter,
wxID_ANY, wxDefaultPosition, wxDefaultSize,
wxLC_REPORT | wxLC_SINGLE_SEL);

    listCtrl->InsertColumn(0, "Name");

    listCtrl->InsertColumn(1, "Size");

    listCtrl->InsertColumn(2, "Type");


    splitter->SplitVertically(treeCtrl,
listCtrl, 200); // Split the window

}


void
MyFrame::OnTreeItemActivated(wxTreeEvent&
event) {

    wxTreeItemId itemId = event.GetItem();

                wxString      path      =
treeCtrl->GetItemText(itemId);
```

```
        PopulateList(listCtrl, path);

    }




void
MyFrame::OnListItemActivated(wxListEvent&
event) {

    long item = event.GetIndex();

                wxString      name      =
listCtrl->GetItemText(item);

                wxString      path      =
treeCtrl->GetItemText(treeCtrl->GetSelectio
n());

            wxString  fullPath  =  path  +
wxFileName::GetPathSeparator() + name;



    if (wxDirExists(fullPath)) {

        PopulateList(listCtrl, fullPath);

            // ... (Optionally expand the
corresponding tree item) ...

        } else {
```

```cpp
            // ... (Open the file with a
default application) ...

    }

}



void     MyFrame::PopulateTree(wxTreeCtrl*
treeCtrl,     const     wxString&     path,
wxTreeItemId parent) {

    wxDir dir(path);

    if (!dir.IsOpened()) return;



    wxString filename;

    bool cont = dir.GetFirst(&filename,
wxEmptyString, wxDIR_DIRS);

    while (cont) {

            wxString fullPath = path +
wxFileName::GetPathSeparator() + filename;

            wxTreeItemId itemId =
treeCtrl->AppendItem(parent, filename);
```

```
        PopulateTree(treeCtrl, fullPath,
itemId);    //    Recursive    call    for
subdirectories

        cont = dir.GetNext(&filename);

    }

}



void      MyFrame::PopulateList(wxListCtrl*
listCtrl, const wxString& path) {

    listCtrl->DeleteAllItems();


    wxDir dir(path);

    if (!dir.IsOpened()) return;


    wxString filename;

        bool cont = dir.GetFirst(&filename,
wxEmptyString, wxDIR_DIRS | wxDIR_FILES);

    while (cont) {

            wxString fullPath = path +
wxFileName::GetPathSeparator() + filename;
```

```
            wxFileName fn(fullPath);



                            long    index    =
listCtrl->InsertItem(listCtrl->GetItemCount
(), filename);

                listCtrl->SetItem(index,  1,
fn.IsDir() ? "" : wxString::Format("%lld",
fn.GetSize()));

                listCtrl->SetItem(index,  2,
fn.IsDir() ? "Directory" : "File");



            cont = dir.GetNext(&filename);

        }

    }
```

**Explanation:**

1. **Structure:** The code uses a wxSplitterWindow to
   divide the window into two parts: a wxTreeCtrl
   on the left to display the directory hierarchy and
   a wxListCtrl on the right to display the contents
   of the selected directory.

2. PopulateTree(): This function recursively populates the tree control with directories starting from the root path ("/").
3. PopulateList(): This function populates the list control with the files and directories in the specified path. It uses wxFileName to get file information like size and type.
4. **Event Handling:**
   - OnTreeItemActivated: When a directory is selected in the tree, this handler calls PopulateList() to display the contents of that directory.
   - OnListItemActivated: When an item is activated in the list (e.g., double-clicked), this handler checks if it's a directory. If it is, it updates the list to display the contents of that directory. If it's a file, you can add code to open it with a default application.

**Key Features:**

- **Cross-Platform Compatibility:** The code uses wxWidgets' file system classes (wxDir, wxFileName) to ensure it works correctly on different operating systems.
- **Recursive Directory Traversal:** The PopulateTree() function uses recursion to traverse the directory structure.

- **File Information:** The list control displays file names, sizes, and types.
- **Basic Navigation:** Users can navigate through directories by clicking on items in the tree or list.

This example provides a basic framework for a cross-platform file explorer. You can extend it further by adding features like:

- **Back and Forward Navigation:** Implement buttons or menu items for navigating back and forward through the directory history.
- **Context Menus:** Add context menus to the tree and list controls for actions like "Open," "Delete," "Rename," etc.
- **File Operations:** Implement file operations like copying, moving, and deleting files.
- **Filtering and Sorting:** Allow users to filter and sort files by name, size, type, or date.
- **Icons:** Display icons for different file types.

# Part III: Qt Development

# Chapter 8: Introduction to Qt

## Core Concepts: Widgets, Layouts, Signals and Slots

Qt is a comprehensive C++ framework for building cross-platform applications, including GUI applications. It offers a rich set of tools and libraries that simplify GUI development and provide a consistent look and feel across different operating systems. This section introduces some of the core concepts in Qt: widgets, layouts, and the signals and slots mechanism.

### 1. Widgets

Widgets are the fundamental building blocks of Qt GUIs. They represent visual elements like buttons, labels, text boxes, list views, and more. Qt provides a vast collection of pre-built widgets, and you can also create your own custom widgets.

- **Common Widgets:**
    - QPushButton: A clickable button.
    - QLabel: A text label.
    - QLineEdit: A single-line text input field.
    - QTextEdit: A multi-line text editor.
    - QListWidget: A list of selectable items.

- QComboBox: A dropdown list of selectable items.
- QCheckBox: A checkbox.
- QRadioButton: A radio button.
- **Creating a Widget:**

C++

```
QPushButton *button = new QPushButton("Click me!", parentWidget);
```

- **Widget Hierarchy:** Widgets are organized in a parent-child hierarchy. The parent widget manages the layout and behavior of its child widgets.

## 2. Layouts

Layouts manage the size and position of widgets within their parent widget. They ensure that your GUI adapts well to different window sizes and screen resolutions.

- **Common Layout Managers:**
  - QHBoxLayout: Arranges widgets horizontally in a row.
  - QVBoxLayout: Arranges widgets vertically in a column.

- o  QGridLayout: Arranges widgets in a grid with rows and columns.
- o  QFormLayout: Arranges widgets in a two-column form with labels and input fields.
- **Using Layouts:**

C++

```cpp
QWidget *window = new QWidget();

QPushButton *button1 = new QPushButton("Button 1");

QPushButton *button2 = new QPushButton("Button 2");


QHBoxLayout *layout = new QHBoxLayout(window);
// Create a horizontal layout

layout->addWidget(button1); // Add widgets to the layout

layout->addWidget(button2);
```

## 3. Signals and Slots

Signals and slots are Qt's mechanism for communication between objects. They provide a type-safe and flexible way to handle events and connect different parts of your application.

- **Signals:** Emitted by Qt objects when a particular event occurs (e.g., button clicked, text changed).
- **Slots:** Member functions that are called in response to a signal.
- **Connecting Signals and Slots:**

C++

```cpp
QObject::connect(sender, &Sender::signalName, receiver, &Receiver::slotName);
```

- **Example:**

C++

```cpp
QPushButton *button = new QPushButton("Click me!");

QLabel *label = new QLabel("Hello!");


QObject::connect(button, &QPushButton::clicked, label, &QLabel::clear);

// When the button is clicked, the label's text is cleared.
```

**Benefits of Signals and Slots:**

- **Loose Coupling:** The sender and receiver objects don't need to know about each other.
- **Type Safety:** The compiler ensures that signals and slots have compatible arguments.
- **Flexibility:** You can connect multiple signals to a single slot, or a single signal to multiple slots.

**Putting it all together:**

Widgets, layouts, and signals and slots are fundamental concepts in Qt GUI programming. Widgets provide the visual elements, layouts arrange them on the screen, and signals and slots handle communication and event handling. Together, they form the foundation for building responsive and interactive Qt applications.

# Building Your First Qt Application with Qt Creator

Qt Creator is the official IDE for Qt development. It provides a user-friendly environment for creating, building, and running Qt applications. This section guides you through the process of building a simple "Hello, World!" application using Qt Creator.

**Step 1: Launch Qt Creator**

If you haven't already, download and install Qt Creator from the official Qt website (qt.io). Once installed, launch Qt Creator.

### Step 2: Create a new project

- Go to **File > New File or Project...**
- Select **Qt Widgets Application** from the **Application** category.
- Click **Choose**.

### Step 3: Configure the project

- **Name:** Give your project a name (e.g., "HelloWorld").
- **Location:** Choose a directory to store your project files.
- **Kit Selection:** Select the appropriate kit for your target platform (this includes the compiler and Qt version).
- Click **Next** and then **Finish**.

### Step 4: Design the user interface

Qt Creator will generate a basic project with a main window (MainWindow). You can design the user interface using Qt Designer, a visual design tool integrated into Qt Creator.

- In the **Projects** pane, open the **Forms** folder and double-click on mainwindow.ui to open it in Qt Designer.
- Drag a QPushButton widget from the **Buttons** section of the **Widget Box** onto the main window.
- Double-click the button and change its text to "Say Hello".

### Step 5: Connect the signal and slot

- Right-click the "Say Hello" button in Qt Designer and select **Go to slot...**.
- Choose the clicked() signal and click **OK**.
- Qt Creator will generate a slot function (on_pushButton_clicked()) in mainwindow.cpp.

### Step 6: Implement the slot function

In mainwindow.cpp, add the following code inside the on_pushButton_clicked() function:

C++

```cpp
#include "mainwindow.h"

#include "ui_mainwindow.h"

#include <QMessageBox>
```

```cpp
MainWindow::MainWindow(QWidget *parent)
    : QMainWindow(parent)
    , ui(new Ui::MainWindow)
{
    ui->setupUi(this);
}


MainWindow::~MainWindow()
{
    delete ui;
}



void MainWindow::on_pushButton_clicked()
{
    QMessageBox::information(this, "Hello", "Hello, world!");
}
```

This code will display a message box with the text "Hello, world!" when the button is clicked.

**Step 7: Build and run**

- Click the **Build** button (or press **Ctrl+B**) to build the project.
- Click the **Run** button (or press **Ctrl+R**) to run the application.

You should see a window with a "Say Hello" button. Clicking the button will display the "Hello, world!" message box.

Congratulations! You've built your first Qt application with Qt Creator. This simple example demonstrates the basic workflow of creating a Qt GUI application, including designing the UI with Qt Designer and connecting signals and slots. You can now expand on this foundation to create more complex and interactive applications.

## Step-by-step guide to using Qt Creator for project creation and design

**Step 1: Launch Qt Creator and Create a New Project**

1. **Open Qt Creator:** Start by opening the Qt Creator IDE. You'll be greeted with a welcome screen.
2. **New Project:** Click on the "New Project" button or go to File > New File or Project....
3. **Choose a Template:** In the "New Project" dialog, you'll see various project templates. For creating a GUI application with widgets, select "Qt Widgets Application" under the "Application" category. Click "Choose."

### Step 2: Configure Project Settings

1. **Project Name and Location:**
   - **Name:** Provide a descriptive name for your project (e.g., "MyGUIApp").
   - **Create in:** Choose the directory where you want to save your project files.
   - Click "Next."
2. **Kit Selection:**
   - **Kit:** Select the appropriate kit for your target platform. A kit defines the compiler, Qt version, and other build settings. If you have multiple kits installed, choose the one that matches your desired environment.
   - Click "Next."
3. **Class Information:**

- ○ **Class name:** This is the name of your main window class (e.g., "MainWindow").
- ○ **Base class:** Qt Creator defaults to QMainWindow, which provides a main application window with a menu bar, toolbars, and a status bar. You can choose other base classes like QWidget for a simpler window.
- ○ **Header file, Source file, Form file:** These fields show the names of the files that will be generated for your main window class.
- ○ Click "Next."

4. **Project Management:**
   - ○ You can choose to use a version control system (e.g., Git) for your project. If you're not using version control, select "None."
   - ○ Click "Finish."

## Step 3: Design the User Interface (UI)

1. **Open Qt Designer:** Qt Creator will generate the necessary files for your project. To design the UI, open the mainwindow.ui file. You can find it in the "Forms" folder in the "Projects" pane. Double-clicking it will open Qt Designer.

2. **Familiarize Yourself with Qt Designer:**

- ○ **Widget Box:** On the left side, you'll find the "Widget Box," which contains all the available Qt widgets.
- ○ **Main Window:** The central area displays your main window where you can drag and drop widgets.
- ○ **Object Inspector:** On the right side, the "Object Inspector" shows the hierarchy of widgets in your UI and their properties.
- ○ **Property Editor:** Below the "Object Inspector," the "Property Editor" allows you to modify the properties of the selected widget.

3. **Add Widgets:** Drag and drop widgets from the "Widget Box" onto your main window. For example, add a QPushButton, a QLabel, and a QLineEdit.

4. **Arrange with Layouts:** Use layouts to arrange your widgets. Drag a layout from the "Layouts" section of the "Widget Box" onto your main window. Then, drag the widgets into the layout to position them.

5. **Customize Widgets:** Select a widget and use the "Property Editor" to change its properties, such as its text, size, color, and object name.

6. **Preview:** Click the "Preview" button in Qt Designer to see how your UI will look when the application runs.

**Step 4: Connect Signals and Slots**

1. **Signals and Slots Editor:** Switch to the "Signals and Slots Editor" mode in Qt Designer (by clicking the appropriate icon in the left sidebar).
2. **Make Connections:** Click and drag from a widget that emits a signal (e.g., the QPushButton) to a widget that has a slot (e.g., the QLabel). This will open a "Configure Connection" dialog.
3. **Choose Signal and Slot:** In the dialog, select the signal you want to connect (e.g., clicked()) and the slot you want to trigger (e.g., clear() to clear the label's text). Click "OK."

**Step 5: Build and Run**

1. **Build the Project:** Click the "Build" button (the hammer icon) in the bottom left corner of Qt Creator to compile your code.
2. **Run the Application:** Click the "Run" button (the green triangle icon) to run your application and see your designed UI in action.

This step-by-step guide provides a comprehensive overview of using Qt Creator for project creation and UI design. By following these steps and exploring the various features of Qt Creator, you can efficiently build and design Qt applications.

# Code samples: A basic calculator application with Qt Designer

**C++**

```cpp
// mainwindow.h

#ifndef MAINWINDOW_H
#define MAINWINDOW_H


#include <QMainWindow>


QT_BEGIN_NAMESPACE

namespace Ui { class MainWindow; }

QT_END_NAMESPACE


class MainWindow : public QMainWindow

{

    Q_OBJECT
```

```cpp
public:

    MainWindow(QWidget *parent = nullptr);

    ~MainWindow();


private slots:

    void on_pushButton_digit_clicked();

    void on_pushButton_operator_clicked();

    void on_pushButton_equal_clicked();

    void on_pushButton_clear_clicked();


private:

    Ui::MainWindow *ui;

    double num1, num2;

    QString currentOperator;
};

#endif // MAINWINDOW_H
```

```cpp
// mainwindow.cpp

#include "mainwindow.h"

#include "ui_mainwindow.h"

#include <QMessageBox>


MainWindow::MainWindow(QWidget *parent)

    : QMainWindow(parent)

    , ui(new Ui::MainWindow)

{

    ui->setupUi(this);


    // Connect digit buttons

                connect(ui->pushButton_0,
&QPushButton::clicked,                    this,
&MainWindow::on_pushButton_digit_clicked);

                connect(ui->pushButton_1,
&QPushButton::clicked,                    this,
&MainWindow::on_pushButton_digit_clicked);

        // ... connect other digit buttons
(2-9) similarly ...
```

```cpp
    // Connect operator buttons

            connect(ui->pushButton_plus,
&QPushButton::clicked,                  this,
&MainWindow::on_pushButton_operator_clicked
);

            connect(ui->pushButton_minus,
&QPushButton::clicked,                  this,
&MainWindow::on_pushButton_operator_clicked
);

    // ... connect other operator buttons
(multiply, divide) similarly ...

}



MainWindow::~MainWindow()

{

    delete ui;

}



void
MainWindow::on_pushButton_digit_clicked()
```

```cpp
{
    QPushButton *button = qobject_cast<QPushButton*>(sender());     // Get the clicked button

    QString digit = button->text();

    QString currentText = ui->lineEdit_display->text();

    ui->lineEdit_display->setText(currentText + digit);

}


void MainWindow::on_pushButton_operator_clicked()

{
    QPushButton *button = qobject_cast<QPushButton*>(sender());

    currentOperator = button->text();

    num1 = ui->lineEdit_display->text().toDouble();

    ui->lineEdit_display->clear();
```

```cpp
}


void
MainWindow::on_pushButton_equal_clicked()

{

                                num2        =
ui->lineEdit_display->text().toDouble();

    double result;


    if (currentOperator == "+") {

        result = num1 + num2;

    } else if (currentOperator == "-") {

        result = num1 - num2;

    } else if (currentOperator == "*") {

        result = num1 * num2;

    } else if (currentOperator == "/") {

        if (num2 == 0) {

                QMessageBox::warning(this,
"Error", "Division by zero!");
```

```
            return;

        }

        result = num1 / num2;

    } else {

        return; // Invalid operator

    }


ui->lineEdit_display->setText(QString::numb
er(result));

}



void
MainWindow::on_pushButton_clear_clicked()

{

    ui->lineEdit_display->clear();

    num1 = 0;

    num2 = 0;

    currentOperator = "";
```

}

**Explanation:**

1. **UI Design (mainwindow.ui):**
   - Use Qt Designer to create the calculator UI with:
     - A QLineEdit for the display.
     - QPushButtons for digits (0-9), operators (+, -, *, /), "=", and "Clear".
     - Arrange the buttons using a QGridLayout.
2. MainWindow **Class:**
   - num1, num2: Store the operands.
   - currentOperator: Stores the current operator.
3. **Slots:**
   - on_pushButton_digit_clicked(): Appends the clicked digit to the display.
   - on_pushButton_operator_clicked(): Stores the first number and the operator.
   - on_pushButton_equal_clicked(): Performs the calculation and displays the result.
   - on_pushButton_clear_clicked(): Clears the display and resets the calculator.

4. **Connections:**
   - In the MainWindow constructor, connect the clicked() signals of all buttons to their respective slots.

**Key Improvements:**

- **Object-Oriented Design:** The calculator logic is encapsulated in the MainWindow class.
- **Clearer Code:** Using Qt Designer simplifies the UI creation and separates it from the code.
- **Extensible:** You can easily add more features (e.g., memory functions, scientific operations) by adding buttons and slots.

This example provides a solid foundation for building a more functional calculator application. You can customize the UI, add more operations, and implement error handling to create a complete calculator.

## Practice: Modifying the calculator to add more functions

Let's make your Qt calculator more functional by adding some common features. Here are a few ideas to get you started:

**1. Decimal Point**

- Add a "." button to the UI.

- Modify the on_pushButton_digit_clicked() slot to handle the decimal point:
  - If the current display text doesn't already contain a ".", append "." to it.

## 2. Backspace

- Add a "Backspace" button to the UI.
- Create a new slot on_pushButton_backspace_clicked():
  - Get the current text from the display.
  - Remove the last character using QString::chopped().
  - Update the display with the modified text.

## 3. Percentage

- Add a "%" button to the UI.
- Create a new slot on_pushButton_percentage_clicked():
  - Get the current number from the display.
  - Divide the number by 100.
  - Update the display with the result.

## 4. Square Root

- Add a "√" button to the UI.
- Create a new slot on_pushButton_sqrt_clicked():
  - Get the current number from the display.
  - Calculate the square root using qSqrt().
  - Update the display with the result.

## 5. Memory Functions

- Add buttons for "M+", "M-", "MR", "MC" (memory plus, minus, recall, clear).
- Add a private member variable double memoryValue to store the memory value.
- Implement the corresponding slots to handle memory operations:
  - on_pushButton_Mplus_clicked(): Add the current number to memoryValue.
  - on_pushButton_Mminus_clicked(): Subtract the current number from memoryValue.
  - on_pushButton_MR_clicked(): Display memoryValue on the display.
  - on_pushButton_MC_clicked(): Clear memoryValue.

## 6. +/- (Change Sign)

- Add a "+/-" button to the UI.
- Create a new slot on_pushButton_changeSign_clicked():
  - Get the current number from the display.
  - Multiply the number by -1.
  - Update the display with the result.

## Example: Adding a Decimal Point

C++

```cpp
void MainWindow::on_pushButton_digit_clicked()

{

                        QPushButton        *button        =
qobject_cast<QPushButton*>(sender());

    QString digit = button->text();

    QString currentText = ui->lineEdit_display->text();


    if (digit == ".") {

            if (!currentText.contains(".")) { // Check if a
decimal point already exists

                ui->lineEdit_display->setText(currentText +
digit);

        }

    } else {

        ui->lineEdit_display->setText(currentText + digit);

    }

}
```

**Remember to:**

- Add the new buttons to your UI in Qt Designer.
- Connect the clicked() signals of the new buttons to their respective slots in the MainWindow constructor.
- Implement the logic for each new function in the corresponding slot.
- Test your calculator thoroughly after adding each new feature.

By adding these functions, you'll create a more versatile and user-friendly calculator application. You can continue to expand its functionality by adding more advanced operations or exploring other features like keyboard input and history tracking.

# Chapter 9: Qt Widgets and Layouts

## Essential Widgets: Buttons, Labels, Line Edits, Combo Boxes

Qt provides a comprehensive collection of widgets for building user interfaces. This section covers some of the most essential widgets you'll use in your Qt applications: buttons, labels, line edits, and combo boxes. You'll learn how to create them, configure their properties, and connect them to signals and slots for interactivity.

**1. Buttons** (QPushButton)

Buttons are used to trigger actions in your application. They can display text, icons, or both.

- **Creation:**

C++

```
QPushButton *button = new QPushButton(parent);
```

- **Setting Text and Icon:**

C++

```
button->setText("Click me!");
```

```cpp
button->setIcon(QIcon(":/images/icon.png"));
```

- **Common Signals:**
    - clicked(): Emitted when the button is clicked.
    - pressed(): Emitted when the button is pressed.
    - released(): Emitted when the button is released.
- **Connecting to a Slot:**

C++

```cpp
connect(button, &QPushButton::clicked, this, &MyClass::onButtonClicked);
```

## 2. Labels (QLabel)

Labels display static or dynamic text. They can also display images.

- **Creation:**

C++

```cpp
QLabel *label = new QLabel(parent);
```

- **Setting Text:**

C++

```
label->setText("This is a label.");
```

- **Displaying an Image:**

C++

```
label->setPixmap(QPixmap(":/images/image.jpg"));
```

- **Properties:**
  - alignment: Controls the text alignment (e.g., Qt::AlignLeft, Qt::AlignCenter).
  - wordWrap: Enables or disables word wrapping.
  - textFormat: Sets the text format (e.g., plain text, HTML).

## 3. Line Edits (QLineEdit)

Line edits allow users to enter and edit a single line of text.

- **Creation:**

C++

QLineEdit *lineEdit = new QLineEdit(parent);

- **Setting Text:**

C++

lineEdit->setText("Initial text");

- **Properties:**
  - placeholderText: Displays placeholder text when the line edit is empty.
  - echoMode: Controls how the text is displayed (e.g., QLineEdit::Normal, QLineEdit::Password).
  - maxLength: Limits the number of characters that can be entered.
- **Common Signals:**
  - textChanged(const QString &text): Emitted when the text changes.
  - returnPressed(): Emitted when Enter is pressed.

**4. Combo Boxes** (QComboBox)

Combo boxes provide a dropdown list of options for the user to select from.

- **Creation:**

C++

QComboBox *comboBox = new QComboBox(parent);

- **Adding Items:**

C++

comboBox->addItem("Option 1");

comboBox->addItem("Option 2");

comboBox->addItems(QStringList() << "Option 3" << "Option 4");

- **Properties:**
  - currentIndex: The index of the currently selected item.
  - currentText: The text of the currently selected item.

- o editable: Allows the user to edit the selected item.
- **Common Signals:**
  - o currentIndexChanged(int index): Emitted when the current index changes.
  - o currentTextChanged(const QString &text): Emitted when the current text changes.

**Example:**

C++

```
// ... in your widget's constructor ...


QPushButton *button = new QPushButton("Submit");

QLabel *nameLabel = new QLabel("Name:");

QLineEdit *nameLineEdit = new QLineEdit();

QComboBox *countryComboBox = new QComboBox();

countryComboBox->addItems(QStringList() << "USA" << "Canada" << "Mexico");


// ... add widgets to a layout ...
```

```
connect(button,        &QPushButton::clicked,        this,
&MyWidget::onSubmit);
```

This example demonstrates how to create and use essential widgets in Qt. You can combine these widgets with layouts, signals, and slots to build interactive and functional user interfaces for your applications.

## Layout Managers: QHBoxLayout, QVBoxLayout, QGridLayout

Layout managers are essential tools in Qt for organizing widgets within a user interface. They control the size and position of widgets, ensuring they are arranged in a visually appealing and functional manner. Qt provides several layout managers, and this section covers three of the most commonly used ones: QHBoxLayout, QVBoxLayout, and QGridLayout.

**1.** QHBoxLayout **(Horizontal Box Layout)**

QHBoxLayout arranges widgets horizontally in a row, from left to right.

- **Creation:**

C++

```cpp
QHBoxLayout *layout = new QHBoxLayout();
```

- **Adding Widgets:**

C++

```cpp
layout->addWidget(widget1);
layout->addWidget(widget2);
layout->addWidget(widget3);
```

- **Spacing and Margins:**
  - setSpacing(int spacing): Sets the spacing between widgets.
  - setContentsMargins(int left, int top, int right, int bottom): Sets the margins around the layout.
- **Example:**

C++

```cpp
QHBoxLayout *layout = new QHBoxLayout();
layout->addWidget(new QPushButton("Button 1"));
```

```
layout->addWidget(new QPushButton("Button 2"));

layout->addWidget(new QPushButton("Button 3"));


QWidget *window = new QWidget();

window->setLayout(layout);

window->show();
```

This will create a window with three buttons arranged horizontally.

## 2. QVBoxLayout (Vertical Box Layout)

QVBoxLayout arranges widgets vertically in a column, from top to bottom.

- **Creation and usage are similar to QHBoxLayout:**

C++

```
QVBoxLayout *layout = new QVBoxLayout();

layout->addWidget(widget1);

layout->addWidget(widget2);
```

// ...

### 3. QGridLayout **(Grid Layout)**

QGridLayout arranges widgets in a grid with rows and columns.

- **Creation:**

C++

```
QGridLayout *layout = new QGridLayout();
```

- **Adding Widgets:**

C++

```
layout->addWidget(widget, row, column, rowSpan, columnSpan, alignment);
```

- row, column: The row and column index where the widget should be placed.
- rowSpan, columnSpan: The number of rows and columns the widget should span.

- alignment: Optional alignment flags (e.g., Qt::AlignTop, Qt::AlignCenter).
- **Example:**

C++

```
QGridLayout *layout = new QGridLayout();

layout->addWidget(new QPushButton("Button 1"), 0, 0);

layout->addWidget(new QPushButton("Button 2"), 0, 1);

layout->addWidget(new QPushButton("Button 3"), 1, 0, 1, 2); // Span 2 columns


QWidget *window = new QWidget();

window->setLayout(layout);

window->show();
```

This will create a grid layout with "Button 3" spanning two columns.

**Important Notes:**

- **Setting the Layout:** After creating a layout and adding widgets to it, you need to set it as the layout for the parent widget using setLayout(layout).

- **Nesting Layouts:** You can nest layouts within each other to create complex arrangements.
- **Stretch Factors:** You can use setColumnStretch(int column, int stretch) and setRowStretch(int row, int stretch) to control how much space rows and columns take up when the window is resized.

By understanding and utilizing these layout managers, you can create well-organized and responsive user interfaces in your Qt applications.

## Using Qt Designer for UI Design

Qt Designer is a powerful visual tool that simplifies the process of creating user interfaces for Qt applications. It allows you to drag and drop widgets, arrange them with layouts, and customize their properties without writing code. This WYSIWYG (What You See Is What You Get) approach makes UI design more intuitive and efficient.

### 1. Accessing Qt Designer

You can access Qt Designer in two ways:

- **Standalone Application:** Qt Designer can be launched as a standalone application from your Qt installation directory.

- **Integrated in Qt Creator:** Qt Designer is integrated into Qt Creator, making it seamless to switch between designing the UI and writing code.

## 2. Qt Designer Interface

Qt Designer's interface consists of:

- **Widget Box:** Contains a categorized list of available Qt widgets.
- **Form Editor:** The central area where you design your UI by dragging and dropping widgets.
- **Object Inspector:** Displays the hierarchy of widgets in your UI.
- **Property Editor:** Allows you to modify the properties of the selected widget.
- **Signals and Slots Editor:** Enables you to connect signals and slots between widgets.
- **Action Editor:** Used for creating and managing actions for menus and toolbars.

## 3. Designing the UI

- **Drag and Drop Widgets:** Drag widgets from the Widget Box onto the Form Editor.
- **Arrange with Layouts:** Use layouts (e.g., QHBoxLayout, QVBoxLayout, QGridLayout) to arrange widgets in a structured manner.

- **Customize Properties:** Select a widget and modify its properties (e.g., text, size, color, object name) in the Property Editor.
- **Set Object Names:** Give meaningful object names to your widgets (e.g., buttonSubmit, labelName) to easily access them in your code.

## 4. Connecting Signals and Slots

- **Signals and Slots Editor:** Switch to the Signals and Slots Editor mode in Qt Designer.
- **Connect Signals and Slots:** Click and drag from a signal-emitting widget to a slot-receiving widget to create a connection.
- **Configure Connection:** In the "Configure Connection" dialog, choose the specific signal and slot to connect.

## 5. Working with Layouts

- **Lay Out Widgets:** Select multiple widgets and apply a layout to them using the **Lay out** options in the toolbar or context menu.
- **Adjust Layout Properties:** Modify layout properties (e.g., spacing, margins) in the Property Editor.
- **Breaking Layouts:** Use the **Break Layout** option to remove a layout from a group of widgets.

### 6. Previewing the UI

- **Preview:** Click the **Preview** button in Qt Designer to see how your UI will look at runtime.
- **Preview with Different Styles:** Choose different styles (e.g., Windows, Fusion) to see how your UI adapts to different platforms.

### 7. Generating Code

- **UI Files:** Qt Designer saves your UI design in .ui files, which are XML-based descriptions of the user interface.
- uic **(User Interface Compiler):** The uic tool compiles .ui files into C++ code that you can integrate into your application.

### Benefits of Using Qt Designer

- **Rapid UI Development:** Quickly create and iterate on UI designs without writing code.
- **Visual Feedback:** See the results of your design changes immediately.
- **Separation of Concerns:** Separates UI design from application logic, making your code more organized and maintainable.
- **Accessibility:** Qt Designer provides features for creating accessible UIs for users with disabilities.

By mastering Qt Designer, you can significantly streamline your UI development workflow and create professional-looking Qt applications with ease.

## Common Mistakes: Overusing Qt Designer and neglecting code-based UI creation

Qt Designer is a fantastic tool for rapid UI prototyping and designing visually appealing interfaces. However, over-reliance on Qt Designer and neglecting code-based UI creation can lead to several drawbacks and limitations in your Qt applications.

**1. Loss of Flexibility**

Qt Designer excels at creating static layouts, but it can be less flexible when dealing with dynamic UIs that need to change at runtime based on user interactions or data.

- **Limitations with Dynamic Content:** If your UI needs to add, remove, or rearrange widgets based on user actions or data updates, doing this solely within Qt Designer can be cumbersome.
- **Complex Logic:** Implementing complex UI logic, such as custom animations, transitions, or interactions that require fine-grained control, might be more challenging or less efficient when relying solely on Qt Designer.

## 2. Reduced Code Understanding

When you rely heavily on Qt Designer, the UI structure and widget properties are defined in .ui files, which are separate from your C++ code. This separation can:

- **Hinder Code Comprehension:** Make it harder for developers to understand the complete picture of the UI and its connections to the application logic.
- **Increase Debugging Difficulty:** Debugging UI-related issues might require switching between Qt Designer and the code, making the process less efficient.

## 3. Potential for "Bloated" UIs

Qt Designer makes it easy to add widgets and layouts, but this can sometimes lead to overly complex and "bloated" UIs with unnecessary elements or inefficient layout hierarchies.

- **Performance Impact:** Overuse of nested layouts or a large number of widgets can negatively impact the performance of your application, especially on resource-constrained devices.
- **Maintainability Issues:** Complex UIs created solely in Qt Designer can be harder to maintain and modify as the application evolves.

## 4. Limited Customization

While Qt Designer offers many customization options, it might not cover all possible use cases. You might encounter situations where you need to create custom widgets or implement specific behaviors that are not readily achievable through Qt Designer's visual interface.

- **Custom Widget Creation:** Creating highly specialized or visually unique widgets often requires code-based implementation for maximum flexibility and control.
- **Advanced Effects:** Implementing advanced visual effects or animations might require direct manipulation of widget properties and rendering through code.

## Best Practices

- **Balance Visual Design and Code:** Use Qt Designer for initial UI prototyping and basic layout design, but don't hesitate to write code for dynamic UI elements, complex logic, and custom widgets.
- **Code Organization:** Keep your UI code well-organized and structured, even when using Qt Designer. Use clear naming conventions and comments to improve readability.

- **Performance Optimization:** Be mindful of the number of widgets and layout complexity when designing your UI. Avoid unnecessary nesting and optimize for performance.
- **Learn Qt's Core:** Develop a strong understanding of Qt's core concepts, including widgets, layouts, and the event system, to effectively combine code-based UI creation with Qt Designer.

By striking a balance between Qt Designer and code-based UI creation, you can leverage the strengths of both approaches. This allows you to build UIs that are visually appealing, flexible, and maintainable.

## Best Practices: Combining Qt Designer with code for flexibility

While Qt Designer simplifies UI design, relying solely on it can limit flexibility. Combining Qt Designer with code allows you to leverage the strengths of both approaches and build more dynamic and adaptable user interfaces. Here are some best practices:

### 1. Use Qt Designer for Basic Structure

Start by using Qt Designer to create the basic structure of your UI.

- **Lay out main elements:** Place the core widgets (buttons, labels, text boxes, etc.) and arrange them using layouts (QHBoxLayout, QVBoxLayout, QGridLayout).
- **Establish visual hierarchy:** Group related widgets using frames (QFrame) or group boxes (QGroupBox) to create a clear visual hierarchy.
- **Set basic properties:** Configure essential properties like widget size, text, and object names.

## 2. Code Dynamic Content

For UI elements that need to change at runtime (e.g., adding or removing widgets, updating data), write code to manipulate the UI.

- **Connect to Data:** Populate list views, tables, or other data-driven widgets by connecting them to your application's data models through code.
- **Create Widgets Dynamically:** Use new to create widgets at runtime based on user actions or application state.
- **Modify Properties Dynamically:** Change widget properties (e.g., visibility, enabled state, text) through code to reflect changes in the application.

## 3. Implement Custom Widgets

When you need specialized functionality or unique visual elements, create custom widgets by subclassing QWidget or other widget classes.

- **Extend Existing Widgets:** Inherit from existing Qt widgets to add custom behavior or modify their appearance.
- **Create from Scratch:** Build completely new widgets with custom painting and event handling.

## 4. Handle Complex Logic

For complex UI logic, such as animations, transitions, or custom interactions, implement the behavior in your code.

- **Animation Framework:** Use Qt's animation framework (QPropertyAnimation, QAnimationGroup) to create smooth animations and transitions.
- **Event Handling:** Connect signals and slots to handle user interactions and trigger UI updates.
- **Custom Painting:** Override the paintEvent() method to create custom drawing and visual effects.

## 5. Maintain Code Clarity

Even when using Qt Designer, keep your code well-organized and readable.

- **Separate UI Logic:** Separate UI-related code from your application's core logic to improve maintainability.
- **Naming Conventions:** Use clear and consistent naming conventions for widgets and UI-related variables.
- **Comments and Documentation:** Add comments to explain complex UI logic and document your custom widgets.

**Example: Dynamically Adding Widgets**

C++

```
// In your widget's class:

QVBoxLayout *layout; // Vertical layout to hold widgets


// ... in the constructor ...

layout = new QVBoxLayout(this);


// ... in a slot that adds a new button ...

QPushButton *newButton = new QPushButton("New Button");
```

```cpp
layout->addWidget(newButton);
```

This example shows how to dynamically add buttons to a vertical layout at runtime.

**Key Benefits**

- **Flexibility:** Create UIs that adapt to user interactions and data changes.
- **Maintainability:** Keep your code organized and easier to understand.
- **Customization:** Build unique and specialized UI elements.
- **Performance:** Optimize UI performance by controlling widget creation and layout complexity.

By combining Qt Designer with code, you can create user interfaces that are both visually appealing and highly functional, providing a rich and engaging experience for your users.

## Code samples: Creating dynamic layouts that adjust to window size

C++

```cpp
#include <QtWidgets>
```

```cpp
class MyWidget : public QWidget
{
    Q_OBJECT


public:
    MyWidget(QWidget *parent = nullptr) :
QWidget(parent)
    {
        // Create widgets
            QLabel *nameLabel = new
QLabel("Name:");

        nameEdit = new QLineEdit();

            QLabel *addressLabel = new
QLabel("Address:");

        addressEdit = new QTextEdit();


        // Create layouts
```

```cpp
        QFormLayout *formLayout = new
QFormLayout();

            formLayout->addRow(nameLabel,
nameEdit);


        mainLayout = new QVBoxLayout(this);

        mainLayout->addLayout(formLayout);


        // Initially hide the address
section

        addressLabel->hide();

        addressEdit->hide();

    }


protected:

    void resizeEvent(QResizeEvent *event)
override

    {

        int width = event->size().width();
```

```cpp
                if (width > 400 &&
!addressEdit->isVisible()) {

        // Window is wide enough, show
the address section`

mainLayout->addWidget(addressLabel);

mainLayout->addWidget(addressEdit);

        addressLabel->show();

        addressEdit->show();

        } else if (width <= 400 &&
addressEdit->isVisible()) {

        // Window is too narrow, hide
the address section

mainLayout->removeWidget(addressLabel);

mainLayout->removeWidget(addressEdit);

        addressLabel->hide();

        addressEdit->hide();
```

```cpp
        }


            QWidget::resizeEvent(event);

    }


private:
    QLineEdit *nameEdit;

    QLabel *addressLabel;

    QTextEdit *addressEdit;

    QVBoxLayout *mainLayout;
};


int main(int argc, char *argv[])
{

    QApplication app(argc, argv);

    MyWidget widget;

    widget.show();

    return app.exec();
```

}

**Explanation:**

1. **Widgets and Layouts:**
   - The code creates two labels (nameLabel, addressLabel), a line edit (nameEdit), and a text edit (addressEdit).
   - A QFormLayout is used to arrange the name label and line edit.
   - A QVBoxLayout (mainLayout) is used as the main layout for the widget.

2. resizeEvent()**:**
   - This event handler is called whenever the widget is resized.
   - It checks the width of the widget (width).
   - If width is greater than 400 and the address section is not visible, it adds the address label and text edit to the mainLayout and shows them.
   - If width is less than or equal to 400 and the address section is visible, it removes the address label and text edit from the mainLayout and hides them.

3. **Dynamic Layout Adjustment:**
   - By adding and removing widgets from the layout in the resizeEvent(), the UI

dynamically adjusts to the available space.

○ When the window is wide enough, the address section is displayed.

○ When the window becomes too narrow, the address section is hidden to save space.

**Key Concepts:**

- **Layout Management:** The code demonstrates how to dynamically manage layouts by adding and removing widgets.

- **Event Handling:** The resizeEvent() is used to respond to window resize events.

- **Responsive Design:** The UI adapts to different window sizes, providing a better user experience.

This example demonstrates a simple way to create dynamic layouts. You can extend this concept to build more complex UIs that adjust to window size, screen orientation, or other factors. You can also explore other Qt layout managers and features to achieve more sophisticated dynamic layout adjustments.

# Practice: Designing a user interface for a media player

Let's apply your knowledge of Qt widgets and layouts to design a user interface for a basic media player. This exercise will challenge you to combine different widgets and arrange them effectively to create a functional and visually appealing media player control panel.

**UI Requirements:**

- **Display Area:** A central area to display the media (video or visualization for audio). You can use a QLabel to represent this initially.
- **Playback Controls:**
  - Play/Pause button
  - Stop button
  - Previous Track button
  - Next Track button
  - Volume slider
  - Seek bar (slider for navigating through the media)
- **Track Information:**
  - Labels to display track title, artist, and album (or similar information)
- **Playlist:**
  - A list widget (QListWidget) to display the playlist.

## Layout Guidelines:

- Use a QVBoxLayout as the main layout to arrange the UI elements vertically.
- Place the display area at the top, taking up most of the vertical space.
- Use a QHBoxLayout to arrange the playback controls horizontally below the display area.
- Group related controls together (e.g., Previous/Next Track buttons, Volume slider and Seek bar).
- Use a QFormLayout or similar layout to display the track information neatly.
- Place the playlist below the playback controls, allowing it to expand vertically.
- Consider adding a menu bar or toolbar for additional functionalities (e.g., File menu for opening media, View menu for visualization options).

## Example Structure:

```cpp
C++

// In your main window class constructor...


// Create widgets
```

```cpp
QLabel *displayLabel = new QLabel(); // For
media display

QPushButton        *playButton        =        new
QPushButton("Play");

// ... create other buttons and widgets ...



// Create layouts

QVBoxLayout        *mainLayout        =        new
QVBoxLayout(this);

QHBoxLayout        *controlsLayout        =        new
QHBoxLayout();

QFormLayout        *trackInfoLayout        =        new
QFormLayout();

// ... create other layouts as needed ...



// Add widgets to layouts

controlsLayout->addWidget(playButton);

// ... add other controls to controlsLayout
...

trackInfoLayout->addRow("Title:",
trackTitleLabel);
```

```
// ... add other track information to
trackInfoLayout ...


// Add layouts to mainLayout

mainLayout->addWidget(displayLabel, 1); //
Stretch factor 1 to allow expansion

mainLayout->addLayout(controlsLayout);

mainLayout->addLayout(trackInfoLayout);

mainLayout->addWidget(playlistWidget);


// Set the main layout

centralWidget()->setLayout(mainLayout);
```

## Additional Considerations:

- **Styling:** Use Qt Style Sheets (QSS) to customize the appearance of your media player (colors, fonts, button styles).
- **Icons:** Add icons to the buttons for a more visual appeal.
- **Functionality:** Remember that this is just the UI design. You'll need to write code to handle the

actual media playback, playlist management, and other functionalities.

- **User Experience:** Think about the user experience and design the UI to be intuitive and easy to use.

This practice exercise will help you solidify your understanding of Qt widgets and layouts. You can further enhance the UI by adding more features, customizing the appearance, and connecting the widgets to your media player logic.

# Chapter 10: Signals and Slots in Depth

## Connecting Signals and Slots

Signals and slots are the backbone of Qt's event handling system and inter-object communication mechanism. They provide a type-safe and flexible way to connect events generated by one object (signals) to functions in another object (slots). This section delves deeper into the intricacies of connecting signals and slots, empowering you to build responsive and interactive Qt applications.

### 1. The connect() Function

The QObject::connect() function is the heart of Qt's signals and slots mechanism. It establishes a connection between a signal and a slot.

C++

```
QObject::connect(sender, &Sender::signal, receiver, &Receiver::slot);
```

- sender: The object that emits the signal.
- &Sender::signal: A pointer to the member function that defines the signal.
- receiver: The object that contains the slot.

- &Receiver::slot: A pointer to the member function that defines the slot.

## 2. Signal and Slot Signatures

For a connection to be valid, the signal and slot must have compatible signatures:

- **Argument Types:** The slot's arguments must match the signal's arguments in type and order. The slot can have fewer arguments than the signal, but it cannot have more.
- **Return Type:** Slots cannot have a return type (they must be void).

## 3. Connection Types

Qt supports different connection types that determine how the signal is delivered to the slot:

- Qt::AutoConnection **(default):** If the sender and receiver are in the same thread, the slot is called directly (synchronously). If they are in different threads, the signal is queued (asynchronously).
- Qt::DirectConnection: The slot is always called directly, even if the sender and receiver are in different threads.
- Qt::QueuedConnection: The signal is always queued, even if the sender and receiver are in the same thread.

- Qt::BlockingQueuedConnection: Similar to Qt::QueuedConnection, but the sender thread blocks until the slot has finished executing. This is mainly used for communication between threads.
- Qt::UniqueConnection: The connection is established only if there isn't already a connection between the signal and the slot.

You can specify the connection type as the fifth argument to the connect() function:

C++

```
QObject::connect(sender, &Sender::signal, receiver, &Receiver::slot, Qt::QueuedConnection);
```

## 4. Overloaded Signals and Slots

If a signal or slot is overloaded (has multiple versions with different arguments), you need to use the QOverload template to specify which overload you want to connect.

C++

```
// Connect to the overload of the signal that takes an int argument
```

```
QObject::connect(sender,
QOverload<int>::of(&Sender::valueChanged),

        receiver, &Receiver::onValueChanged);
```

## 5. Lambda Expressions as Slots

You can use lambda expressions as slots, providing a concise way to define the slot's behavior directly within the connect() function.

C++

```
QObject::connect(button, &QPushButton::clicked, this,
[this](){

    // Code to execute when the button is clicked

});
```

## 6. Disconnecting Signals and Slots

You can disconnect a signal and slot using the disconnect() function.

C++

QObject::disconnect(sender, &Sender::signal, receiver, &Receiver::slot);

## 7. Advanced Connection Options

- Qt::UniqueConnection: Ensures that only one connection exists between the signal and the slot.
- connect() **return value:** The connect() function returns a QMetaObject::Connection object that you can use to disconnect the connection later.

## 8. Best Practices

- **Use descriptive signal and slot names:** This makes your code more readable and understandable.
- **Choose the appropriate connection type:** Consider the threading model of your application when choosing the connection type.
- **Avoid circular connections:** Circular connections can lead to infinite loops.
- **Use** disconnect() **when necessary:** Disconnect signals and slots when they are no longer needed to prevent memory leaks and unexpected behavior.

By mastering the nuances of connecting signals and slots, you can build robust and responsive Qt applications with well-defined communication pathways between objects. This mechanism is crucial for creating interactive user interfaces and handling events efficiently.

## Custom Signals and Slots

While Qt provides a wide range of built-in signals and slots for its standard widgets, you can define your own custom signals and slots to handle application-specific events and communication between your own objects. This enables you to create more modular, reusable, and responsive Qt applications.

### 1. Defining Custom Signals

- **Use the** signals **keyword:** Declare custom signals within the signals: section of your class definition.
- **Signal Signature:** Specify the signal's name and arguments (if any).
- **No Implementation:** Signals are declared without an implementation. Qt's meta-object compiler (MOC) generates the necessary code behind the scenes.

C++

class MyCustomWidget : public QWidget

```
{

    Q_OBJECT


signals:

    void valueChanged(int newValue); // Signal with an
int argument

     void stateChanged(bool newState); // Signal with a
bool argument

    void customEvent(); // Signal with no arguments


public:

    // ... constructor and other members ...

};
```

## 2. Defining Custom Slots

- **Use the** slots **keyword:** Declare custom slots
  within the public slots: or private slots: section of
  your class definition.
- **Slot Signature:** Specify the slot's name and
  arguments (if any). The slot's arguments must be

compatible with the signal it will be connected to.

- **Implementation:** Provide an implementation for your slot, defining the actions to be performed when the signal is emitted.

C++

```cpp
class MyCustomWidget : public QWidget
{
  Q_OBJECT

public slots:
  void onValueChanged(int newValue) {
    // ... handle the valueChanged signal ...
  }

private slots:
  void updateDisplay(bool newState) {
    // ... handle the stateChanged signal ...
  }
```

public:

```cpp
    // ... constructor and other members ...
};
```

## 3. Emitting Signals

- **Use the** emit **keyword:** Emit a signal from your object to notify connected slots about an event or state change.
- **Provide Arguments:** Pass any necessary arguments to the signal.

C++

```cpp
void MyCustomWidget::someFunction() {

    // ... some code that changes the widget's value ...

    emit valueChanged(newValue); // Emit the signal with the new value

}
```

## 4. Connecting Custom Signals and Slots

- **Use** QObject::connect(): Connect your custom signals and slots just like you would with built-in signals and slots.

C++

MyCustomWidget *widget1 = new MyCustomWidget();

MyCustomWidget *widget2 = new MyCustomWidget();

QObject::connect(widget1, &MyCustomWidget::valueChanged,

widget2, &MyCustomWidget::onValueChanged);

## 5. Benefits of Custom Signals and Slots

- **Modularity:** Decouple objects and improve code organization by defining clear communication channels.
- **Reusability:** Create reusable components that can be easily integrated into different parts of your application.
- **Maintainability:** Make your code easier to understand and maintain by separating concerns and defining clear event handling logic.

- **Extensibility:** Extend the functionality of your application by adding new signals and slots as needed.

**Example: A Custom Slider Widget**

C++

```cpp
class MySlider : public QWidget
{
    Q_OBJECT

signals:
    void valueChanged(int newValue);

public:
    // ... constructor and other members ...

private:
    int m_value;
};
```

// ... in MySlider's implementation ...

```cpp
void MySlider::mouseMoveEvent(QMouseEvent *event) {
    // ... calculate new slider value based on mouse position ...
    m_value = newValue;
    emit valueChanged(m_value); // Emit the custom signal
    update(); // Redraw the slider
}
```

This example shows a custom slider widget that emits a valueChanged signal whenever its value is changed. You can then connect this signal to slots in other objects to respond to slider movements.

By defining custom signals and slots, you can create more flexible and responsive Qt applications with well-defined communication pathways between your own objects. This is a powerful technique for building complex and interactive user interfaces.

## Event Filters

Event filters in Qt provide a powerful mechanism to intercept and handle events before they reach their intended target widget. This allows you to customize event processing, implement application-wide behaviors, or even debug event flow.

### 1. The eventFilter() **Function**

To create an event filter, you need to implement the eventFilter() function in a class that inherits from QObject. This function takes two arguments:

- watched: The object that the event filter is installed on.
- event: The event object.

C++

```
class MyEventFilter : public QObject

{

    Q_OBJECT

public:
```

```cpp
    bool eventFilter(QObject *watched, QEvent *event)
override {

    // ... filter the event ...

    }
};
```

## 2. Installing an Event Filter

Use the installEventFilter() method of the QObject you want to monitor to install the event filter.

C++

```cpp
MyEventFilter *filter = new MyEventFilter(this); // Create an instance of the filter

button->installEventFilter(filter); // Install the filter on the button
```

## 3. Filtering Events

Inside the eventFilter() function, you can examine the event object and decide how to handle it.

- **Event Type:** Use event->type() to get the event type (e.g., QEvent::MouseButtonPress, QEvent::KeyPress).
- **Event Object:** Cast the event pointer to the specific event type to access its properties (e.g., static_cast<QMouseEvent*>(event)->pos()).
- **Accept or Reject:** Return true from eventFilter() to prevent the event from being processed further. Return false to allow the event to propagate to the target widget.

**4. Example: Blocking Escape Key**

C++

```
bool MyEventFilter::eventFilter(QObject *watched,
QEvent *event) {

  if (event->type() == QEvent::KeyPress) {

                    QKeyEvent *keyEvent =
static_cast<QKeyEvent*>(event);

    if (keyEvent->key() == Qt::Key_Escape) {

        // ... handle Escape key press (e.g., display a
message) ...

        return true; // Block the Escape key

    }
```

```
    }

    return QObject::eventFilter(watched, event); // Pass
other events through

}
```

## 5. Application-Wide Event Filters

You can install an event filter on the QApplication object
to filter events for all widgets in your application.

C++

```
QApplication app(argc, argv);

MyEventFilter *filter = new MyEventFilter();

app.installEventFilter(filter);
```

## 6. Removing an Event Filter

Use the removeEventFilter() method to remove an event
filter.

C++

```
button->removeEventFilter(filter);
```

**Benefits of Event Filters**

- **Centralized Event Handling:** Implement common event handling logic in one place.
- **Custom Behavior:** Modify or block events before they reach the target widget.
- **Debugging:** Inspect events to understand event flow and debug issues.
- **Code Reusability:** Create reusable event filters that can be applied to different widgets.

**Important Notes**

- **Performance:** Be mindful of the performance impact of event filters, especially if you install them on many widgets or at the application level.
- **Event Propagation:** Understand how events propagate through the widget hierarchy and how event filters can affect this propagation.

By mastering event filters, you can gain fine-grained control over event handling in your Qt applications and create more sophisticated and interactive user interfaces.

## Code samples: Building a custom signal to notify of data changes

C++

```cpp
#include <QObject>

#include <QString>


class DataModel : public QObject

{

    Q_OBJECT


public:

    DataModel(QObject *parent = nullptr) :
QObject(parent), m_data("Initial data") {}


    QString data() const { return m_data; }

    void setData(const QString &newData) {

        if (m_data != newData) {

            m_data = newData;

            emit dataChanged(m_data); //
Emit the custom signal

        }

    }
```

```cpp
signals:

    void dataChanged(const QString
&newData); // Custom signal


private:

    QString m_data;

};




// Example usage in another class

#include <QLabel>


class MyWidget : public QWidget

{

    Q_OBJECT


public:
```

```cpp
    MyWidget(QWidget *parent = nullptr) :
QWidget(parent)

    {

        model = new DataModel(this);

        label = new QLabel(model->data(),
this);



                                connect(model,
&DataModel::dataChanged,            label,
&QLabel::setText);

        // ... other UI setup ...

    }



private slots:

    void onButtonClicked() {

        // ... some action that changes the
data ...

            model->setData("New  data  from
button click");

    }
```

```
private:

    DataModel *model;

    QLabel *label;

};
```

## Explanation:

1. DataModel **Class:**
   - m_data: Stores the data.
   - data(): Getter function for the data.
   - setData(): Setter function for the data.
     - It checks if the new data is different from the current data.
     - If the data has changed, it updates m_data and emits the dataChanged signal with the new data.
   - dataChanged(const QString &newData): A custom signal that is emitted when the data changes.
2. MyWidget **Class:**
   - model: An instance of the DataModel class.
   - label: A QLabel to display the data.

- Connection: The connect() function connects the dataChanged signal of the model to the setText slot of the label. This means that whenever the data in the model changes, the label's text will be automatically updated.
- onButtonClicked(): This example slot function simulates some action that changes the data in the model by calling model->setData().

**Key Concepts:**

- **Custom Signals:** The dataChanged signal is a custom signal defined in the DataModel class to notify other objects about data changes.
- **Signal Emission:** The emit keyword is used to emit the signal when the data is modified.
- **Connecting to Slots:** The connect() function connects the custom signal to the setText slot of the QLabel, ensuring that the UI is updated automatically when the data changes.

This example demonstrates how to create and use a custom signal to notify other parts of your application about data changes. This pattern is essential for building responsive and data-driven Qt applications. You can adapt this code to create custom signals for various events or state changes in your own classes.

# Practice: Implementing a custom event filter for a specific widget

C++

```cpp
#include <QtWidgets>


// Custom event filter class

class MouseClickLogger : public QObject

{

    Q_OBJECT
public:

        MouseClickLogger(QObject *parent =
nullptr) : QObject(parent) {}


        bool eventFilter(QObject *watched,
QEvent *event) override {

                if (event->type() ==
QEvent::MouseButtonPress) {

                QMouseEvent *mouseEvent =
static_cast<QMouseEvent*>(event);
```

```cpp
            qDebug() << "Mouse click on" <<
watched << "at" << mouseEvent->pos();

            // You can add more specific
actions here, like

            // checking which button was
clicked, etc.

        }

                                      return
QObject::eventFilter(watched,  event);   //
Pass other events through

    }

};



// Widget  where  we  want  to  install  the
filter

class MyWidget : public QWidget

{

    Q_OBJECT


public:
```

```cpp
    MyWidget(QWidget *parent = nullptr) :
QWidget(parent)

    {

        QPushButton *button = new
QPushButton("Click Me!", this);

        // ... other widget setup ...


        MouseClickLogger *logger = new
MouseClickLogger(this);

        button->installEventFilter(logger);
// Install the filter on the button

    }

};


int main(int argc, char *argv[])

{

    QApplication app(argc, argv);

    MyWidget widget;

    widget.show();
```

```
    return app.exec();

}
```

**Explanation:**

1. MouseClickLogger **Class:**
   - This class inherits from QObject and overrides the eventFilter() function.
   - In eventFilter(), it checks if the event type is QEvent::MouseButtonPress.
   - If it is a mouse press event, it casts the event to QMouseEvent and prints information about the click (the watched object and the click position).
   - It then returns false to allow the event to propagate to the button (so the button still performs its normal click action).

2. MyWidget **Class:**
   - This is a simple widget with a QPushButton.
   - In the constructor, it creates an instance of MouseClickLogger and installs it as an event filter on the button using button->installEventFilter(logger).

**How it Works:**

- When you click the button in MyWidget, the eventFilter() function of the MouseClickLogger object will be called **before** the button's own event handler.
- The filter logs the mouse click information.
- Since the filter returns false, the event continues to propagate to the button, and the button behaves normally.

**Key Concepts:**

- **Event Filtering:** This example demonstrates how to intercept and process events before they reach the target widget.
- **Custom Event Handling:** You can add custom logic within the eventFilter() function to perform specific actions based on the event.
- **Selective Filtering:** The filter only logs mouse click events and allows other events to pass through.

This practice exercise provides a basic example of implementing a custom event filter. You can extend this to create more complex filters that:

- Filter different types of events (e.g., key presses, mouse movements).
- Modify event properties before passing them on.
- Perform different actions depending on the event details (e.g., which mouse button was clicked).

- Implement application-wide event filtering by installing the filter on the QApplication object.

# Chapter 11: Advanced Qt Topics

## Model-View Programming with Qt

Qt's Model-View framework offers a powerful and flexible approach to managing and displaying data in your GUI applications. It separates the data (model) from the way it is presented (view), allowing for greater customization, efficiency, and maintainability. This section explores the key concepts and components of Model-View programming in Qt.

### 1. The Model-View Architecture

The Model-View architecture is based on the separation of concerns principle. It divides the handling of data into three distinct roles:

- **Model:** Provides a standardized interface to access and manipulate data, regardless of its underlying structure or storage mechanism.
- **View:** Displays the data provided by the model in a specific format (e.g., list, table, tree).
- **Delegate (Optional):** Customizes the rendering and editing of individual items in the view.

### 2. Benefits of Model-View Programming

- **Data Agnostic:** Views are independent of the underlying data structure, allowing you to use the same view with different data sources.
- **Flexibility:** Easily customize the presentation of data without affecting the model or the underlying data.
- **Efficiency:** Optimized for displaying large datasets by only accessing and rendering the visible data.
- **Code Reusability:** Create reusable models and views that can be combined in different ways.

**3. Models (**QAbstractItemModel**)**

The QAbstractItemModel class is the base class for all models in Qt. It defines the standard interface that views use to access data.

- **Key Concepts:**
    - **Items:** Data is represented as a hierarchical structure of items.
    - **Roles:** Each item can have multiple roles, representing different aspects of the data (e.g., Qt::DisplayRole, Qt::EditRole, Qt::ToolTipRole).
    - **Indexes:** QModelIndex objects are used to identify and access individual items in the model.
- **Implementing a Model:**

- Subclass QAbstractItemModel: Implement the necessary functions to provide data to the view (e.g., data(), rowCount(), columnCount(), index(), parent()).
- **Data Storage:** Choose a suitable data structure to store your data (e.g., lists, arrays, trees).
- **Signal Emission:** Emit signals (e.g., dataChanged, rowsInserted, rowsRemoved) to notify the view about changes in the data.

## 4. Views

Qt provides several standard view classes:

- QListView: Displays data as a list.
- QTableView: Displays data as a table with rows and columns.
- QTreeView: Displays data as a hierarchical tree.
- **Using Views:**
  - **Create a View:** Create an instance of the desired view class.
  - **Set the Model:** Use setModel() to associate the view with a model.
  - **Customization:** Customize the view's appearance and behavior through properties and signals.

## 5. Delegates (QAbstractItemDelegate)

Delegates are optional components that control the rendering and editing of individual items in the view.

- **Customizing Appearance:** Define how items are painted in the view (e.g., using colors, fonts, icons).
- **Providing Editors:** Create custom editors for specific data types (e.g., a date picker for date values).
- **Handling User Interaction:** Handle user input and update the model accordingly.

## 6. Example: A Simple List Model

C++

```cpp
// Custom model for a string list

class StringListModel : public QStringListModel

{

  Q_OBJECT

public:

    StringListModel(QObject *parent = nullptr) :
QStringListModel(parent) {}
```

```
    // ... custom functions to add, remove, or modify
strings ...

};
```

```
// In your widget:

StringListModel *model = new StringListModel(this);

model->setStringList(QStringList() << "Item 1" <<
"Item 2" << "Item 3");
```

```
QListView *listView = new QListView(this);

listView->setModel(model);
```

This example demonstrates a simple list model that stores a list of strings. The QListView is used to display the data provided by the model.

By understanding and applying the Model-View framework, you can create Qt applications that efficiently manage and display data in a structured and flexible way. This architecture promotes code reusability, maintainability, and scalability, making it ideal for applications with complex data requirements.

# Graphics and Painting with QPainter

Qt's 2D graphics engine revolves around the QPainter class. It provides a powerful and versatile toolset for drawing various graphical elements, from simple shapes to complex images and text, on different paint devices. This section explores the essentials of using QPainter to create custom graphics and visual effects in your Qt applications.

## 1. The QPainter Class

QPainter is the core class for performing drawing operations in Qt. It provides functions for drawing:

- **Shapes:** Lines, rectangles, ellipses, arcs, polygons, and Bezier curves.
- **Images:** Loading and drawing images from files or pixmaps.
- **Text:** Rendering text with different fonts and styles.
- **Other Elements:** Points, paths, and gradients.

## 2. Creating a QPainter Object

To start drawing, you need to create a QPainter object and associate it with a paint device.

C++

```
QPainter painter(this); // Create a QPainter on a widget
```

- **Paint Devices:** QPainter can draw on various paint devices, including:
  - QWidget: For drawing on widgets.
  - QPixmap: For drawing on off-screen pixmaps.
  - QImage: For drawing on in-memory images.
  - QPrinter: For printing graphics.

## 3. Drawing Basics

- **Pens:** Define the style and color of lines and outlines.
  - QPen pen(Qt::red, 2, Qt::SolidLine); // Red pen with width 2
  - painter.setPen(pen);
- **Brushes:** Define the fill pattern and color of shapes.
  - QBrush brush(Qt::blue, Qt::Dense4Pattern); // Blue brush with a pattern
  - painter.setBrush(brush);
- **Drawing Functions:**
  - drawLine(x1, y1, x2, y2): Draws a line.

- drawRect(x, y, width, height): Draws a rectangle.
- drawEllipse(x, y, width, height): Draws an ellipse.
- drawText(x, y, text): Draws text.

## 4. Coordinate System

QPainter uses a coordinate system where the top-left corner of the paint device is (0, 0). The x-axis increases to the right, and the y-axis increases downwards.

## 5. Transformations

QPainter supports transformations to rotate, scale, and translate the coordinate system.

- rotate(angle): Rotates the coordinate system by the given angle.
- scale(sx, sy): Scales the coordinate system by the given factors.
- translate(dx, dy): Translates the coordinate system by the given offsets.

## 6. Clipping

Clipping allows you to restrict drawing to a specific region of the paint device.

- setClipRect(rect): Sets a rectangular clipping region.

## 7. Rendering Hints

Rendering hints can be used to improve the quality of the rendered graphics.

- setRenderHint(QPainter::Antialiasing): Enables antialiasing for smoother edges.
- setRenderHint(QPainter::TextAntialiasing): Enables antialiasing for text.

## 8. Example: Drawing a Simple Shape

C++

```cpp
void MyWidget::paintEvent(QPaintEvent *event) {

    QPainter painter(this);


    painter.setPen(QPen(Qt::green, 5, Qt::DashLine));
                    painter.setBrush(QBrush(Qt::yellow,
Qt::SolidPattern));


    painter.drawRect(10, 10, 100, 80);
}
```

This code draws a green dashed rectangle filled with yellow on the widget.

### 9. Beyond the Basics

QPainter offers many more features, including:

- **Gradients:** Linear and radial gradients for smooth color transitions.
- **Paths:** Complex shapes defined by a sequence of lines and curves.
- **Composition Modes:** Control how colors are blended together.
- **Antialiasing:** Smooth out jagged edges for better visual quality.

By mastering QPainter and its capabilities, you can create custom graphics and visual effects that enhance the user experience and functionality of your Qt applications.

## QML and Qt Quick for Modern UIs

While traditional Qt widgets provide a robust foundation for building user interfaces, QML and Qt Quick offer a more modern and declarative approach, particularly well-suited for creating dynamic, fluid, and visually rich applications. This section introduces QML and Qt Quick, highlighting their key features and benefits for modern UI development.

# 1. What is QML?

QML (Qt Meta-object Language) is a declarative language designed for creating user interfaces. It uses a JavaScript-like syntax with extensions for defining UI elements, their properties, and their relationships. QML code is easy to read and write, making it ideal for rapid prototyping and UI design.

# 2. What is Qt Quick?

Qt Quick is a module within the Qt framework that provides a high-performance rendering engine and a set of pre-built QML elements for building user interfaces. It leverages the power of OpenGL (or other graphics APIs) for hardware-accelerated rendering, resulting in smooth animations and fluid transitions.

# 3. Key Features of QML and Qt Quick

- **Declarative Syntax:** Describe the UI in a declarative way, focusing on what the UI should look like rather than how to achieve it.
- **Property Bindings:** Dynamically update UI elements based on changes in properties or data.
- **Animations and Transitions:** Easily create animations and transitions for a more engaging user experience.
- **JavaScript Integration:** Use JavaScript for scripting and handling events.

- **Visual Design Tools:** Qt Design Studio and Qt Creator provide visual editors for designing QML-based UIs.
- **Cross-Platform Compatibility:** Build UIs that run on various platforms (desktop, mobile, embedded).

## 4. QML Basic Syntax

- **Elements:** Basic building blocks of a QML UI (e.g., Rectangle, Text, Image).
- **Properties:** Define the appearance and behavior of elements (e.g., width, height, color, text).
- **Property Bindings:** Dynamically update properties based on expressions or data changes (e.g., width: parent.width / 2).
- **Signals and Handlers:** Handle events and user interactions (e.g., onClicked: { // do something }).

## 5. Qt Quick Elements

Qt Quick provides a rich set of pre-built elements for common UI components:

- **Basic Elements:** Rectangle, Text, Image, MouseArea.
- **Controls:** Button, Slider, CheckBox, RadioButton, ComboBox.
- **Layouts:** Row, Column, Grid, Flow.

- **Other Elements:** ListView, GridView, PathView, Animation, Transition.

## 6. Example: A Simple QML Rectangle

QML

```
import QtQuick 2.0

Rectangle {
    width: 200
    height: 100
    color: "red"

    Text {
        text: "Hello, QML!"
        anchors.centerIn: parent
    }
}
```

This code creates a red rectangle with the text "Hello, QML!" centered inside it.

## 7. Integrating QML with C++

You can integrate QML and C++ code to leverage the strengths of both:

- **Expose C++ Data and Functions to QML:** Use QObject-derived classes and the QML_ELEMENT macro to make C++ data and functions accessible from QML.
- **Call QML Functions from C++:** Use the QQuickView or QQuickWindow class to load QML code and interact with it from C++.

## 8. Benefits of QML and Qt Quick

- **Rapid UI Development:** Quickly prototype and build UIs with the declarative syntax and visual tools.
- **Fluid and Dynamic UIs:** Create modern UIs with smooth animations and transitions.
- **Improved Designer-Developer Workflow:** QML's clear syntax and visual tools facilitate collaboration between designers and developers.
- **Cross-Platform Reach:** Build applications that run on various platforms with a consistent look and feel.

QML and Qt Quick are powerful tools for creating modern and engaging user interfaces. By combining them with your C++ expertise, you can build Qt applications that are both visually appealing and highly functional.

## Networking and Database Connectivity

Modern applications often require interaction with networks and databases to access remote resources, store and retrieve data, and communicate with other systems. Qt provides comprehensive tools and APIs for networking and database connectivity, enabling you to build connected and data-driven applications.

### 1. Networking with Qt

Qt's networking classes offer a high-level and cross-platform way to perform network operations, such as:

- **TCP Sockets:** Establish connections between clients and servers using TCP (Transmission Control Protocol).
  - QTcpSocket: Represents a TCP socket.
  - QTcpServer: Listens for incoming connections.
- **UDP Sockets:** Send and receive datagrams using UDP (User Datagram Protocol).

- ○ QUdpSocket: Represents a UDP socket.
- **HTTP and FTP:** Interact with web servers and FTP servers.
  - ○ QNetworkAccessManager: Manages network requests and responses.
  - ○ QNetworkRequest: Represents a network request.
  - ○ QNetworkReply: Represents a network reply.
- **Other Networking Features:**
  - ○ **DNS Lookup:** Resolve hostnames to IP addresses.
  - ○ **Network Proxies:** Connect to networks through proxy servers.
  - ○ **SSL Support:** Secure communication using SSL/TLS.

## 2. Database Connectivity with Qt

Qt's SQL module provides a platform-independent and database-agnostic way to interact with various database systems.

- **Supported Databases:** Qt supports a wide range of databases, including:
  - ○ SQLite
  - ○ MySQL
  - ○ PostgreSQL
  - ○ Oracle

- o Microsoft SQL Server
- **Key Classes:**
  - o QSqlDatabase: Represents a database connection.
  - o QSqlQuery: Executes SQL statements.
  - o QSqlTableModel: Provides an interface to access and manipulate data in a table.
  - o QSqlQueryModel: Displays the results of an SQL query.
- **Connecting to a Database:**

C++

```
QSqlDatabase db = QSqlDatabase::addDatabase("QMYSQL"); // Choose the database driver

db.setHostName("localhost");

db.setDatabaseName("mydatabase");

db.setUserName("user");

db.setPassword("password");


if (db.open()) {

    // Connection successful

} else {
```

```
    // Connection failed

}
```

- **Executing SQL Queries:**

C++

```cpp
QSqlQuery query;

query.exec("SELECT * FROM mytable");


while (query.next()) {

    QString name = query.value("name").toString();

    // ... process data ...

}
```

## 3. Model-View with Databases

You can use Qt's Model-View framework with databases to efficiently display and manage data in your GUI applications.

- **QSqlTableModel:** Provides a model interface to a database table, allowing you to easily display and edit data in a QTableView.

## 4. Example: A Simple Network Client

C++

```
QTcpSocket *socket = new QTcpSocket(this);

connect(socket, &QTcpSocket::connected, this, &MyWidget::onConnected);

connect(socket, &QTcpSocket::readyRead, this, &MyWidget::onReadyRead);


socket->connectToHost("localhost", 1234);


void MyWidget::onConnected() {

    // ... send data to the server ...

}


void MyWidget::onReadyRead() {

    // ... read data from the server ...
```

```
}
```

This code creates a TCP socket and connects it to a server. The onConnected slot is called when the connection is established, and the onReadyRead slot is called when data is available to read.

**5. Best Practices**

- **Asynchronous Operations:** Use asynchronous network and database operations to avoid blocking the GUI thread.
- **Error Handling:** Implement proper error handling to gracefully handle network and database errors.
- **Security:** Consider security implications when working with networks and databases, especially when handling sensitive data.
- **Threading:** Use threads to perform long-running network or database operations in the background.

By utilizing Qt's networking and database classes, you can build connected and data-driven applications that interact with remote resources and manage persistent data.

# Real-world usage examples: Creating a chat application with Qt

C++

```cpp
// chatclient.h
#ifndef CHATCLIENT_H
#define CHATCLIENT_H

#include <QWidget>
#include <QTcpSocket>

QT_BEGIN_NAMESPACE
namespace Ui { class ChatClient; }
QT_END_NAMESPACE

class ChatClient : public QWidget
{
    Q_OBJECT
```

```cpp
public:

    ChatClient(QWidget *parent = nullptr);

    ~ChatClient();


private slots:

    void on_pushButton_connect_clicked();

    void on_pushButton_send_clicked();

    void onConnected();

    void onReadyRead();

    void onDisconnected();


private:

    Ui::ChatClient *ui;

    QTcpSocket *socket;

    QString username;
};

#endif // CHATCLIENT_H
```

```cpp
// chatclient.cpp

#include "chatclient.h"

#include "ui_chatclient.h"

#include <QMessageBox>

#include <QHostAddress>


ChatClient::ChatClient(QWidget *parent)

    : QWidget(parent)

    , ui(new Ui::ChatClient)

    , socket(new QTcpSocket(this))

{

    ui->setupUi(this);

    connect(socket, &QTcpSocket::connected,
this, &ChatClient::onConnected);

    connect(socket, &QTcpSocket::readyRead,
this, &ChatClient::onReadyRead);
```

```cpp
    connect(socket,
&QTcpSocket::disconnected,                this,
&ChatClient::onDisconnected);

}


ChatClient::~ChatClient()

{

    delete ui;

}


void
ChatClient::on_pushButton_connect_clicked()

{

    QString     host     =
ui->lineEdit_host->text();

    quint16     port     =
ui->lineEdit_port->text().toInt();

    username     =
ui->lineEdit_username->text();
```

```cpp
    socket->connectToHost(QHostAddress(host),
port);

}



void
ChatClient::on_pushButton_send_clicked()

{

                QString      message      =
ui->lineEdit_message->text();

    if (!message.isEmpty()) {

                socket->write(QString("%1:
%2\n").arg(username).arg(message).toUtf8())
;

        ui->lineEdit_message->clear();

    }

}



void ChatClient::onConnected()

{
```

```cpp
    ui->pushButton_connect->setEnabled(false);

    ui->pushButton_send->setEnabled(true);

    ui->textEdit_chat->append("Connected to
server.");

}


void ChatClient::onReadyRead()

{

    while (socket->canReadLine()) {

                        QString   line   =
QString::fromUtf8(socket->readLine()).trimm
ed();

        ui->textEdit_chat->append(line);

    }

}


void ChatClient::onDisconnected()

{
```

```
ui->pushButton_connect->setEnabled(true);

    ui->pushButton_send->setEnabled(false);

        ui->textEdit_chat->append("Disconnected
from server.");

}
```

## Explanation:

1. **UI Design (chatclient.ui):**
   - Use Qt Designer to create the chat client UI with:
     - QLineEdits for host, port, and username.
     - A QTextEdit to display the chat messages.
     - QPushButtons for "Connect" and "Send".
2. ChatClient **Class:**
   - socket: A QTcpSocket for network communication.
   - username: Stores the user's name.
3. **Slots:**
   - on_pushButton_connect_clicked(): Connects to the server using the provided host, port, and username.

- ○ on_pushButton_send_clicked(): Sends the message entered by the user.
- ○ onConnected(): Handles the connected() signal from the socket.
- ○ onReadyRead(): Handles the readyRead() signal from the socket, reading and displaying incoming messages.
- ○ onDisconnected(): Handles the disconnected() signal from the socket.

4. **Network Communication:**
   - ○ The QTcpSocket is used to connect to the server and send/receive messages.
   - ○ The readLine() function is used to read incoming messages line by line.

**Key Concepts:**

- **TCP Sockets:** The chat application uses TCP sockets for reliable communication between the client and server.
- **Signals and Slots:** Qt's signals and slots mechanism is used to handle network events and user interactions.
- **Text Streams:** The QTextStream class can be used to format and send messages over the socket.

This example provides a basic framework for a chat client. You can extend it further by adding features like:

- **User Authentication:** Implement a login system for user authentication.
- **Private Messaging:** Allow users to send private messages to other users.
- **File Transfer:** Enable file sharing between users.
- **Emojis and Rich Text:** Support emojis and rich text formatting in messages.
- **User Lists:** Display a list of connected users.

# Part IV: Putting It All Together

# Chapter 12: Building Real-World Applications

## Project 1: A Cross-Platform Text Editor

This chapter marks the culmination of your journey through C++ GUI development with wxWidgets and Qt. You'll now apply your accumulated knowledge to build a real-world application: a cross-platform text editor. This project will challenge you to integrate various concepts, including widget usage, layout management, event handling, file I/O, and potentially even advanced features like syntax highlighting.

**Project Goals:**

- **Core Functionality:**
  - Create a text editing area (wxTextCtrl in wxWidgets, QTextEdit in Qt).
  - Implement basic editing operations (cut, copy, paste, undo, redo).
  - Open, save, and create new text files.
  - Provide a menu bar with common options (File, Edit, View, Help).
- **Cross-Platform Compatibility:**
  - Ensure the editor works seamlessly on Windows, macOS, and Linux.

- Use platform-independent file handling mechanisms.
- **User-Friendly Interface:**
  - Design a clean and intuitive layout.
  - Provide clear visual feedback for user actions.
  - Consider accessibility features for users with disabilities.
- **Optional Advanced Features:**
  - Font selection and formatting.
  - Find and replace functionality.
  - Line numbers.
  - Syntax highlighting for different programming languages.
  - Printing support.

## Implementation Guidelines:

1. **Choose Your Framework:** Decide whether you want to use wxWidgets or Qt for this project.
2. **Design the UI:** Plan the layout of your text editor. Consider using a wxSplitterWindow (wxWidgets) or QSplitter (Qt) to create resizable panes for the text editing area and potentially other elements like a file explorer or project view.
3. **Implement Core Functionality:**
   - Create the main window and the text editing area.

- Add a menu bar with File, Edit, and other relevant menus.
- Implement menu items for opening, saving, and creating new files.
- Connect menu items to appropriate event handlers.
- Use file dialogs (wxFileDialog in wxWidgets, QFileDialog in Qt) for file selection.

4. **Handle User Input:**
   - Capture keyboard events for text input and editing commands.
   - Implement cut, copy, paste, undo, and redo functionality.

5. **Cross-Platform Considerations:**
   - Use platform-independent file paths and line ending conventions.
   - Test your editor on different operating systems to ensure compatibility.

6. **Optional Advanced Features:**
   - Implement font selection, find and replace, line numbers, or other features as desired.
   - For syntax highlighting, you might need to use a more advanced text control like wxStyledTextCtrl (wxWidgets) or integrate a third-party library.

**Example Structure (wxWidgets):**

C++

```cpp
// ... (In MyFrame class) ...

wxTextCtrl* textArea;

void MyFrame::OnOpen(wxCommandEvent& event) {
    wxFileDialog openFileDialog(this, _("Open File"), "",
"", "Text files (*.txt)|*.txt", wxFD_OPEN |
wxFD_FILE_MUST_EXIST);
    if (openFileDialog.ShowModal() == wxID_OK) {
        textArea->LoadFile(openFileDialog.GetPath());
    }
}

void MyFrame::OnSave(wxCommandEvent& event) {
    // ... (Implement save functionality) ...
}
```

// ... (Event handlers for other menu items) ...

**Example Structure (Qt):**

C++

// ... (In MainWindow class) ...

```cpp
QTextEdit *textArea;

void MainWindow::on_actionOpen_triggered() {
    QString fileName = QFileDialog::getOpenFileName(this, "Open File", "", "Text files (*.txt)");
    if (!fileName.isEmpty()) {
        QFile file(fileName);
        if (file.open(QIODevice::ReadOnly | QIODevice::Text)) {
            textArea->setPlainText(file.readAll());
        }
    }
}
```

```
        }

    }


void MainWindow::on_actionSave_triggered() {

    // ... (Implement save functionality) ...

    }



    // ... (Slots for other actions) ...
```

This project provides an opportunity to synthesize your knowledge and build a practical application that you can use and share. Don't hesitate to explore different features and customize the editor to your liking. The process of building this text editor will solidify your understanding of C++ GUI development and prepare you for tackling even more complex projects in the future.

### Project guidelines: Feature list, design considerations, implementation steps

This section provides detailed guidelines for building your cross-platform text editor project, including a feature list, design considerations, and implementation steps.

## 1. Feature List

- **Essential Features:**
  - Text editing area with basic formatting (bold, italic, underline).
  - Menu bar with standard options (File, Edit, Format, View, Help).
  - File operations (New, Open, Save, Save As).
  - Editing operations (Cut, Copy, Paste, Undo, Redo).
  - Font selection dialog.
  - Find and Replace functionality.
  - Status bar with line/column information and file encoding.
- **Optional Advanced Features:**
  - Line numbers.
  - Syntax highlighting for specific programming languages.
  - Printing support.
  - Auto-completion.
  - Code folding.
  - Tabbed interface for multiple documents.

## 2. Design Considerations

- **User Interface:**

- Layout: Use a clear and intuitive layout with a main text editing area and a menu bar. Consider using a splitter window to allow resizing of different areas (e.g., a side panel for file exploration).
- Icons: Use icons for menu items and toolbar buttons to enhance visual clarity.
- Accessibility: Consider accessibility features for users with disabilities (e.g., keyboard navigation, screen reader compatibility).

- **Cross-Platform Compatibility:**
  - File Handling: Use platform-independent file paths and line ending conventions.
  - Appearance: Strive for a consistent look and feel across different operating systems while respecting platform-specific conventions.
  - Testing: Thoroughly test your editor on Windows, macOS, and Linux to ensure compatibility.
- **Code Structure:**
  - Modularity: Organize your code into logical modules (e.g., UI, document management, text editing operations).
  - Object-Oriented Design: Use classes and objects to represent different components of the editor.

○ **Code Reusability:** Create reusable components for common tasks (e.g., file handling, text manipulation).

## 3. Implementation Steps

- **Step 1: Project Setup**
    ○ Choose your framework (wxWidgets or Qt).
    ○ Create a new project in your chosen IDE.
    ○ Set up the basic application structure (main window, application class).
- **Step 2: UI Design**
    ○ Design the main window layout using Qt Designer (Qt) or by creating widgets and sizers programmatically (wxWidgets).
    ○ Add a menu bar with File, Edit, Format, View, and Help menus.
    ○ Create a text editing area (wxTextCtrl or QTextEdit).
    ○ Add a status bar to display information.
- **Step 3: Core Functionality**
    ○ Implement File menu items (New, Open, Save, Save As).
    ○ Use file dialogs for opening and saving files.
    ○ Implement Edit menu items (Cut, Copy, Paste, Undo, Redo).

- Connect menu items to appropriate event handlers or slots.
- **Step 4: Text Editing**
  - Handle keyboard events for text input and editing commands.
  - Implement basic text formatting (bold, italic, underline).
  - Add a font selection dialog.
- **Step 5: Find and Replace**
  - Create a dialog for Find and Replace functionality.
  - Implement search and replace operations within the text area.
- **Step 6: Cross-Platform Compatibility**
  - Ensure file paths are handled correctly on different platforms.
  - Test your editor on Windows, macOS, and Linux.
- **Step 7: Optional Advanced Features**
  - Implement line numbers, syntax highlighting, printing, or other advanced features as desired.
- **Step 8: Testing and Refinement**
  - Thoroughly test your text editor for functionality, usability, and cross-platform compatibility.
  - Refine the UI and code based on testing feedback.

**Remember to:**

- Consult the documentation for your chosen framework (wxWidgets or Qt) for details on specific classes and methods.
- Break down the project into smaller, manageable tasks.
- Test your code frequently and use debugging tools to identify and fix errors.
- Consider using version control (e.g., Git) to track your code changes.

By following these guidelines and applying your knowledge of C++ GUI development, you can successfully build a functional and cross-platform text editor. This project will not only reinforce your skills but also provide you with a valuable tool that you can use and customize for your own needs.

## Project 2: A Data Visualization Tool

This project challenges you to create a data visualization tool that allows users to import data and generate various types of charts and graphs. This application will combine your GUI programming skills with data handling and visualization techniques.

**Project Goals**

- **Core Functionality:**

- Import data from various formats (CSV, Excel, etc.).
- Display data in a tabular format.
- Generate different chart types (bar charts, line charts, pie charts, scatter plots, etc.).
- Customize chart appearance (colors, labels, titles).
- Export charts as images.

- **User-Friendly Interface:**
  - Design an intuitive interface for data import, chart selection, and customization.
  - Provide clear visual feedback and error handling.

- **Optional Advanced Features:**
  - Support for different data sources (databases, online APIs).
  - Interactive charts with zooming, panning, and tooltips.
  - Data analysis features (e.g., calculating statistics, trend lines).
  - Dashboard creation with multiple charts.

## Project Guidelines

1. **Choose Your Framework and Libraries:**
   - Select either wxWidgets or Qt for the GUI framework.

- Choose a suitable data visualization library:
  - **wxWidgets:** wxFreeChart, wxMathPlot
  - **Qt:** QCustomPlot, Qwt

2. **Design the UI:**
   - Create a main window with areas for:
     - Data import and preview.
     - Chart selection and customization.
     - Chart display.
   - Use appropriate layouts to arrange the UI elements.

3. **Implement Data Import:**
   - Handle different data formats (CSV, Excel).
   - Use appropriate data structures to store the imported data.
   - Display the data in a tabular format for preview.

4. **Implement Chart Generation:**
   - Allow users to select different chart types.
   - Use the chosen data visualization library to generate charts based on the selected data and chart type.
   - Provide options for customizing chart appearance (colors, labels, titles).

5. **Handle User Interaction:**

- Connect UI elements (buttons, sliders, etc.) to appropriate event handlers or slots.
- Allow users to interact with the charts (e.g., zooming, panning).
- Provide feedback and error handling for user actions.
6. **Optional Advanced Features:**
   - Implement support for different data sources, interactive charts, or data analysis features as desired.

**Example Structure (Qt with QCustomPlot)**

C++

```
// ... (In your main window class) ...


QCustomPlot *customPlot; // Widget for displaying the chart

QVector<double> xData, yData; // Data for the chart


void
MainWindow::on_pushButton_generateChart_clicked()
{
```

```
// ... (Get data from the UI or data model) ...


customPlot->addGraph();

customPlot->graph(0)->setData(xData, yData);

customPlot->xAxis->setLabel("X Axis");

customPlot->yAxis->setLabel("Y Axis");

customPlot->rescaleAxes();

customPlot->replot();

}
```

**Key Considerations:**

- **Data Handling:** Choose appropriate data structures to store and manipulate the data.
- **Chart Customization:** Provide options for users to customize the appearance of the charts.
- **Performance:** Optimize for performance, especially when dealing with large datasets or complex visualizations.
- **User Experience:** Design the UI to be intuitive and easy to use.

This project provides a practical application of your C++ GUI skills in the context of data visualization. By combining your knowledge of widgets, layouts, event handling, and data visualization libraries, you can create a valuable tool for exploring and presenting data in a meaningful way.

Project guidelines: Choosing appropriate charts, handling data input, user interaction

This section provides more specific guidance on key aspects of building your data visualization tool: choosing appropriate charts, handling data input, and designing user interactions.

## 1. Choosing Appropriate Charts

Selecting the right chart type is crucial for effectively conveying the information hidden within your data. Here's a guide to help you choose:

- **Bar Chart:**
    - **Use for:** Comparing different categories or groups.
    - **Variations:** Vertical, horizontal, grouped, stacked.
    - **Example:** Comparing sales figures for different products.
- **Line Chart:**

- **Use for:** Showing trends over time or continuous data.
- **Example:** Visualizing stock prices over a period.
- **Pie Chart:**
  - **Use for:** Showing proportions of a whole.
  - **Example:** Representing market share of different companies.
- **Scatter Plot:**
  - **Use for:** Showing the relationship between two variables.
  - **Example:** Analyzing the correlation between advertising spending and sales.
- **Area Chart:**
  - **Use for:** Similar to line charts, but also showing the magnitude of change over time.
  - **Example:** Visualizing the cumulative growth of investments.
- **Other Chart Types:**
  - **Bubble Chart:** A variation of a scatter plot where the size of the bubble represents a third variable.
  - **Heatmap:** Visualizing data using color variations.
  - **Treemap:** Displaying hierarchical data as nested rectangles.

## 2. Handling Data Input

- **Data Formats:**
  - **CSV (Comma-Separated Values):** A common and simple format. Use libraries like wxCSV (wxWidgets) or Qt's text stream classes to parse CSV data.
  - **Excel:** Use libraries like libxlsxwriter (wxWidgets) or QXlsx (Qt) to read and write Excel files.
  - **Databases:** Use Qt's SQL module (QSqlDatabase, QSqlQuery) to connect to databases and retrieve data.
- **Data Validation:**
  - **Data Types:** Ensure that the imported data is of the correct type (e.g., numeric, text, date).
  - **Missing Values:** Handle missing or invalid data appropriately.
  - **Data Range:** Check for outliers or unexpected values that might affect the visualization.
- **Data Transformation:**
  - **Cleaning:** Clean the data by removing duplicates, correcting errors, and handling missing values.
  - **Aggregation:** Aggregate data by grouping or summarizing it to create more meaningful visualizations.

- ○ **Normalization:** Normalize data to a common scale for better comparison.

## 3. User Interaction

- **Chart Selection:**
  - ○ Provide a clear and intuitive way for users to select the desired chart type (e.g., dropdown list, buttons).
  - ○ Display appropriate options for customization based on the selected chart type.
- **Chart Customization:**
  - ○ **Colors:** Allow users to choose colors for different data series or chart elements.
  - ○ **Labels:** Enable customization of axis labels, titles, and legends.
  - ○ **Data Selection:** Allow users to select specific data columns or rows for visualization.
- **Interactive Charts:**
  - ○ **Zooming and Panning:** Implement zooming and panning to allow users to explore the data in more detail.
  - ○ **Tooltips:** Display tooltips with data values when the user hovers over chart elements.
  - ○ **Data Filtering:** Enable filtering of data to focus on specific subsets.

- **Exporting Charts:**
  - **Image Formats:** Allow users to export charts as images (PNG, JPG, PDF).
  - **Data Export:** Provide options for exporting the underlying data in different formats.

**Example: Handling CSV Input (Qt)**

C++

```cpp
void MainWindow::on_actionOpen_triggered() {

    QString fileName = QFileDialog::getOpenFileName(this, "Open CSV File", "", "CSV Files (*.csv)");

    if (!fileName.isEmpty()) {

    QFile file(fileName);

        if (file.open(QIODevice::ReadOnly | QIODevice::Text)) {

        QTextStream in(&file);

        while (!in.atEnd()) {

            QString line = in.readLine();

            QStringList data = line.split(",");
```

```
        // ... (Process and store the data) ...

    }

  }

}

}
```

By carefully considering these guidelines and applying your C++ GUI programming skills, you can create a powerful and user-friendly data visualization tool. This project will enhance your ability to handle data, generate insightful visualizations, and design interactive user interfaces.

## Project 3: A Networked Game

This project takes you into the exciting realm of networked applications by building a simple networked game. This will involve combining your GUI development skills with network programming concepts to create an interactive experience where multiple players can connect and play together over a network.

**Project Goals**

- **Core Functionality:**

- **Client-Server Architecture:** Implement a client-server model where multiple clients can connect to a central server.
- **Game Logic:** Develop the core game logic, including game rules, player actions, and win/lose conditions.
- **Network Communication:** Handle network communication between the clients and the server, including sending and receiving game state updates.
- **User Interface:** Create a user interface for displaying the game board, player information, and controls.

- **Game Choice:**
  - Choose a simple game that is suitable for network implementation (e.g., Tic-Tac-Toe, checkers, a card game).
- **Optional Advanced Features:**
  - **Chat Functionality:** Allow players to communicate with each other through a chat system.
  - **Lobby System:** Create a lobby where players can see available games and join them.
  - **User Authentication:** Implement a login system for player authentication.
  - **Game Statistics:** Track and display game statistics (e.g., wins, losses, scores).

**Project Guidelines**

1. **Choose Your Framework and Networking Library:**
   - Select either wxWidgets or Qt for the GUI framework.
   - Use the networking classes provided by your chosen framework (e.g., QTcpSocket, QTcpServer in Qt) or consider a cross-platform networking library like Boost.Asio.

2. **Design the Game Architecture:**
   - **Client-Server Model:** Define the roles of the client and server in the game.
   - **Game State:** Determine how the game state will be represented and synchronized between the clients and the server.
   - **Network Protocol:** Design a simple protocol for communication between the clients and the server (e.g., using text-based messages or a binary format).

3. **Implement the Server:**
   - **Handle Connections:** Accept connections from multiple clients.
   - **Manage Game State:** Maintain the authoritative game state and update it based on client actions.

- Broadcast Updates: Send game state updates to all connected clients.
4. **Implement the Client:**
   - Connect to Server: Allow the user to connect to the server using a specified IP address and port.
   - Send Actions: Send player actions to the server.
   - Receive Updates: Receive game state updates from the server and update the UI accordingly.
5. **Design the User Interface:**
   - Game Board: Create a visual representation of the game board.
   - Player Information: Display information about the players (e.g., names, scores).
   - Controls: Provide controls for player actions (e.g., making moves, sending messages).
6. **Optional Advanced Features:**
   - Implement chat functionality, a lobby system, or other advanced features as desired.

**Example Structure (Qt)**

C++

// ... (In the server class) ...

```cpp
QTcpServer *server;

QList<QTcpSocket*> clients;


void Server::onNewConnection() {
    QTcpSocket    *client = server->nextPendingConnection();

    clients.append(client);

    // ... (Handle client connection) ...

}


// ... (In the client class) ...


QTcpSocket *socket;


void Client::on_pushButton_send_clicked() {
    QString message = ui->lineEdit_message->text();

    socket->write(message.toUtf8());
```

```
}


void Client::onReadyRead() {

    // ... (Read and process data from the server) ...

}
```

## Key Considerations:

- **Network Latency:** Handle network latency to ensure a smooth gaming experience.
- **Synchronization:** Synchronize the game state between the clients and the server to prevent inconsistencies.
- **Security:** Consider security measures to prevent cheating or unauthorized access.
- **Scalability:** Design the server to handle a reasonable number of concurrent clients.

This project combines your GUI development skills with network programming to create an interactive and engaging multiplayer game. It will deepen your understanding of client-server architecture, network communication, and game development concepts.

Let's delve deeper into the key aspects of building your networked game, providing more specific guidance on client-server architecture, game logic, and user interface design.

## 1. Client-Server Architecture

- **Server Responsibilities:**
  - **Game Logic:** The server is the authoritative source for the game state. It enforces the rules, validates player actions, and updates the game state accordingly.
  - **Client Management:** Handles client connections, disconnections, and communication.
  - **Data Persistence (Optional):** May store game data (e.g., player accounts, scores, game history) in a database.
- **Client Responsibilities:**
  - **User Input:** Gather user input (e.g., mouse clicks, keyboard input) and send it to the server as game actions.
  - **Rendering:** Render the game state visually, including the game board, players, and other relevant information.

- **User Interface:** Provide a user-friendly interface for interacting with the game.
- **Communication:**
  - **Reliable Protocol:** Use a reliable protocol like TCP (Transmission Control Protocol) to ensure that all game actions and updates are delivered without loss.
  - **Message Format:** Define a clear message format for communication between the client and server (e.g., using JSON or a custom binary format).
  - **Efficient Updates:** Optimize network traffic by only sending necessary updates (e.g., changes in the game state, player actions).

## 2. Game Logic

- **Game Choice:**
  - **Simplicity:** Choose a relatively simple game with well-defined rules and a manageable state space (e.g., Tic-Tac-Toe, checkers, a simple card game).
  - **Turn-Based:** Turn-based games are generally easier to implement for networked play than real-time games.
- **Game State:**

- ○ **Data Structures:** Use appropriate data structures to represent the game state (e.g., arrays, lists, objects).
- ○ **Serialization:** Implement serialization (converting the game state to a format that can be sent over the network) and deserialization (converting the received data back into the game state).
- **Game Rules:**
  - ○ **Validation:** Implement logic on the server to validate player actions according to the game rules.
  - ○ **Win/Lose Conditions:** Define the conditions for winning or losing the game.
- **Example (Tic-Tac-Toe):**
  - ○ **Game State:** A 2D array to represent the game board (empty, X, or O).
  - ○ **Player Actions:** Players send their moves (row and column) to the server.
  - ○ **Validation:** The server checks if the move is valid (empty cell) and updates the board.
  - ○ **Win Condition:** The server checks for three in a row (horizontally, vertically, or diagonally).

## 3. User Interface Design

- **Game Board:**
  - **Visual Representation:** Use appropriate widgets (e.g., labels, images, custom drawing) to represent the game board visually.
  - **Interactive Elements:** Allow players to interact with the board (e.g., clicking on cells to make moves).
- **Player Information:**
  - **Display:** Show player names, scores, or other relevant information.
  - **Turns:** Clearly indicate whose turn it is.
- **Controls:**
  - **Actions:** Provide buttons or other controls for player actions (e.g., "Make Move," "Resign," "Chat").
  - **Feedback:** Provide visual feedback for user actions (e.g., highlighting the selected cell, displaying messages).
- **Chat (Optional):**
  - **Text Input:** Allow players to type messages.
  - **Message Display:** Display chat messages in a separate area.
- **Example (Tic-Tac-Toe):**
  - **Game Board:** A 3x3 grid of buttons.
  - **Player Information:** Labels to display player names and current scores.

- ○ **Controls:** No additional controls needed (players click on the grid buttons to make moves).

By carefully considering these guidelines and applying your C++ GUI development skills, you can create a fun and engaging networked game. This project will enhance your understanding of client-server architecture, network programming, and game development principles.

# Chapter 13: Deployment and Best Practices

## Packaging and Distributing Your Applications (Windows, macOS, Linux)

Creating a great application is only half the battle. To reach your users, you need to package and distribute your application effectively. This involves bundling your executable and necessary resources into a format that users can easily install and run on their respective operating systems. This section explores the intricacies of packaging and distributing your C++ GUI applications built with wxWidgets or Qt on Windows, macOS, and Linux.

### 1. Understanding the Challenges

Cross-platform deployment presents unique challenges:

- **Dependencies:** Your application might depend on external libraries (wxWidgets, Qt, or others). You need to ensure these dependencies are included or available on the target system.
- **Platform Differences:** Each operating system has its own conventions for application packaging and installation.

- **User Experience:** The installation process should be smooth and user-friendly.

## 2. Deployment Strategies

- **Static Linking:** Link all dependencies statically into your executable, creating a single, self-contained file. This simplifies distribution but can result in larger file sizes.
- **Dynamic Linking:** Link dependencies dynamically, requiring them to be present on the target system. This reduces file size but adds complexity to the installation process.
- **Bundling Dependencies:** Include necessary dependencies within your application's package.
- **Installation Packages:** Create platform-specific installation packages (e.g., MSI for Windows, DMG for macOS, DEB or RPM for Linux) that handle dependency installation and system integration.

## 3. Platform-Specific Packaging

- **Windows:**
  - **MSI (Microsoft Installer):** The standard format for Windows installers. Use tools like WiX Toolset or Visual Studio Installer Projects to create MSI packages.
  - **Inno Setup:** A popular free tool for creating installers.

- Consider using an installer framework that handles dependencies and registry entries.
- **macOS:**
  - **DMG (Disk Image):** The standard format for distributing macOS applications. Create a DMG file containing your application bundle (.app).
  - **Xcode:** Use Xcode to create and sign your application bundle.
  - **Sign your application with a Developer ID to comply with macOS security requirements.**
- **Linux:**
  - **DEB (Debian Package):** The standard format for Debian-based distributions (e.g., Ubuntu, Debian).
  - **RPM (Red Hat Package Manager):** The standard format for Red Hat-based distributions (e.g., Fedora, CentOS).
  - **Use packaging tools like** dpkg **(DEB) or** rpm **(RPM) to create packages.**
  - **Consider creating packages for different distributions and architectures.**

## 4. Distribution Channels

- **Your Website:** Host your application on your website for direct download.
- **App Stores:** Distribute your application through platform-specific app stores (e.g., Microsoft Store, Mac App Store, Snapcraft).
- **Package Managers:** Make your application available through package managers (e.g., APT for Debian/Ubuntu, Homebrew for macOS).
- **Third-Party Websites:** Use third-party websites (e.g., SourceForge, GitHub) to host and distribute your application.

## 5. Best Practices

- **Clear Installation Instructions:** Provide clear and concise installation instructions for each platform.
- **Versioning:** Use a consistent versioning scheme (e.g., semantic versioning) to track releases.
- **Code Signing:** Sign your application code to ensure its authenticity and integrity.
- **Testing:** Thoroughly test your installation process on different platforms and configurations.
- **Updates:** Provide a mechanism for users to update your application to newer versions.

**Example: Creating a Simple Installer with Inno Setup (Windows)**

Code snippet

```
[Setup]
AppName=My Application
AppVersion=1.0
DefaultDirName={pf}\My Application
OutputBaseFilename=MyApplicationSetup

[Files]
Source: "myapp.exe"; DestDir: "{app}"
Source: "readme.txt"; DestDir: "{app}"

[Run]
Filename: "{app}\myapp.exe"; Description: "Launch My Application"; Flags: nowait postinstall
```

This Inno Setup script creates a basic installer for a Windows application. It defines the application name, version, installation directory, and includes the executable and a readme file.

By carefully considering these aspects of packaging and distribution, you can ensure that your C++ GUI applications reach your target audience effectively and provide a smooth user experience.

## Code Optimization Techniques for GUI Applications

Optimizing the performance of your GUI applications is crucial for providing a smooth and responsive user experience. While C++ is inherently a performant language, GUI applications often involve complex interactions, data processing, and rendering, which can lead to performance bottlenecks if not handled carefully. This section explores various code optimization techniques specifically tailored for GUI applications, helping you create applications that are both efficient and enjoyable to use.

### 1. Profiling and Identifying Bottlenecks

Before diving into optimization, it's essential to identify the performance bottlenecks in your code. Profiling tools can help you pinpoint the areas that consume the most time or resources.

- **Profilers:** Use profiling tools like gprof (GNU profiler), Valgrind (with Callgrind), or Qt

Creator's built-in profiler to analyze your application's performance.

- **Focus on Hotspots:** Identify the functions or code sections that are called most frequently or take the longest to execute. These are your primary targets for optimization.

## 2. Algorithm and Data Structure Optimization

Choosing the right algorithms and data structures can significantly impact performance, especially when dealing with large datasets or complex operations.

- **Efficient Algorithms:** Select algorithms with lower time complexity for critical operations.
- **Appropriate Data Structures:** Use data structures that provide efficient access and manipulation for your specific needs (e.g., hash maps for fast lookups, trees for ordered data).

## 3. Minimize Widget Redrawing

GUI applications spend a significant amount of time redrawing widgets. Minimizing unnecessary redrawing can improve performance.

- **Update Only When Necessary:** Avoid redrawing the entire UI when only a small part has changed.

- **Use** update() **Instead of** repaint()**:** update() schedules a paint event, allowing Qt to optimize redrawing by combining multiple paint events into one.
- **Double Buffering:** Use double buffering to reduce flicker and improve the visual smoothness of animations and updates.

### 4. Efficient Event Handling

Event handling can be a source of overhead if not managed efficiently.

- **Avoid Blocking the Event Loop:** Don't perform long-running operations in event handlers. Use threads or asynchronous operations to avoid blocking the UI.
- **Optimize Event Filters:** If you use event filters, ensure they are as efficient as possible and only filter the necessary events.

### 5. Memory Management

Efficient memory management is crucial for optimal performance.

- **Avoid Memory Leaks:** Use tools like Valgrind to detect and fix memory leaks.

- **Minimize Dynamic Allocation:** If possible, use stack allocation or object pools to reduce the overhead of dynamic memory allocation.

## 6. Optimize for Specific Platforms

Consider platform-specific optimizations when targeting different operating systems.

- **Native APIs:** For performance-critical tasks, you might consider using native APIs directly.
- **Hardware Acceleration:** Utilize hardware acceleration features (e.g., OpenGL) for graphics-intensive applications.

## 7. Other Optimization Techniques

- **Lazy Loading:** Load resources (images, data) only when needed.
- **Caching:** Cache frequently accessed data to avoid redundant calculations or data retrieval.
- **Code Profiling:** Regularly profile your code to identify and address new performance bottlenecks as your application evolves.

### Example: Using Threads for Long-Running Tasks

C++

```
// In your widget's class:
```

```
void MyWidget::onButtonClicked() {

    QtConcurrent::run([this](){

        // Perform long-running task in a separate thread

        // ...


        // Update the UI on the main thread using signals
and slots

        emit resultReady(result);

    });

}
```

This code uses Qt's QtConcurrent::run() to execute a long-running task in a separate thread, preventing it from blocking the UI.

By applying these code optimization techniques and continuously profiling your application, you can create GUI applications that are responsive, efficient, and provide a delightful user experience. Remember that optimization is an iterative process, and it's essential to strike a balance between performance and code maintainability.

# Testing and Debugging Strategies

Thorough testing and effective debugging are essential practices in GUI application development. They ensure that your application functions correctly, provides a positive user experience, and remains stable and reliable. This section explores various testing and debugging strategies specifically tailored for GUI applications, helping you deliver high-quality software.

## 1. Testing Strategies

- **Unit Testing:** Test individual components (widgets, classes, functions) in isolation to verify their correct behavior.
    - **Frameworks:** Use unit testing frameworks like Google Test or Qt Test to write and execute unit tests.
    - **Focus on Logic:** Focus on testing the logic and functionality of your code, rather than the visual aspects of the UI.
- **Integration Testing:** Test the interaction between different components to ensure they work together correctly.
    - **UI Interactions:** Test how different widgets interact and communicate with each other.
    - **Data Flow:** Verify the correct flow of data between components.

- **System Testing:** Test the entire application as a whole, simulating real-world usage scenarios.
    - ○ **User Scenarios:** Create test cases that cover common user interactions and workflows.
    - ○ **Edge Cases:** Test edge cases and boundary conditions to ensure robustness.
- **Regression Testing:** Re-run tests after code changes to ensure that new code doesn't introduce regressions or break existing functionality.
    - ○ **Automated Tests:** Automate regression tests to save time and effort.
- **User Acceptance Testing (UAT):** Involve actual users in testing the application to get feedback on usability and identify real-world issues.

## 2. Debugging Techniques

- **Debugging Tools:**
    - ○ **Debuggers:** Use debuggers like GDB (GNU Debugger) or Qt Creator's debugger to step through code, inspect variables, and set breakpoints.
    - ○ **Logging:** Add logging statements to your code to track program execution and identify errors.

- Memory **Debuggers:** Use tools like Valgrind to detect memory leaks and other memory-related errors.
- **Debugging Strategies:**
  - **Reproduce the Bug:** Clearly identify the steps to reproduce the bug consistently.
  - **Isolate the Problem:** Narrow down the scope of the problem by systematically eliminating potential causes.
  - **Inspect the Code:** Carefully examine the code around the suspected area for logic errors, incorrect assumptions, or unexpected behavior.
  - **Use Breakpoints:** Set breakpoints in your code to pause execution and inspect the program state at specific points.
  - **Print Debugging:** Use qDebug() (Qt) or wxLogMessage() (wxWidgets) to print values and messages to the console or a log file.
  - **Step Through the Code:** Step through the code line by line using the debugger to observe the execution flow and identify the point of failure.
  - **Inspect Variables:** Inspect the values of variables at different points in the execution to understand their state and identify inconsistencies.

## 3. GUI-Specific Debugging

- **Event Handling:** Use debugging tools to trace the flow of events in your application and ensure that they are being handled correctly.
- **Widget Hierarchy:** Inspect the widget hierarchy to understand the relationships between widgets and identify potential layout or rendering issues.
- **Visual Debugging:** Use Qt's "Widget Inspector" or similar tools to inspect the properties and state of widgets at runtime.

## 4. Best Practices

- **Write Testable Code:** Design your code with testability in mind. Use modularity and dependency injection to make it easier to test individual components.
- **Test Early and Often:** Integrate testing into your development workflow from the beginning and test your code frequently.
- **Automate Tests:** Automate as many tests as possible to save time and ensure consistency.
- **Use Assertions:** Use assertions (assert() in C++) to check for invalid conditions and catch errors early.
- **Learn Debugging Tools:** Become proficient with debugging tools to quickly identify and fix bugs.

By combining these testing and debugging strategies, you can significantly improve the quality and reliability of your GUI applications. Remember that testing and debugging are ongoing processes throughout the development lifecycle, and they are crucial for delivering software that meets user expectations and functions flawlessly.

## Writing Maintainable and Scalable GUI Code

As your GUI applications grow in complexity, it becomes crucial to write code that is maintainable and scalable. Maintainable code is easy to understand, modify, and extend, while scalable code can handle increasing amounts of data and user interactions without performance degradation. This section explores best practices and techniques for writing maintainable and scalable GUI code in C++, whether you're using wxWidgets or Qt.

### 1. Code Organization

- **Modularity:** Break down your code into smaller, self-contained modules with clear responsibilities. This improves code readability and makes it easier to locate and fix bugs.
- **Separation of Concerns:** Separate the UI logic from the application's core logic. This promotes

code reusability and makes it easier to modify the UI without affecting the underlying functionality.

- **Classes and Objects:** Use object-oriented programming principles to encapsulate data and behavior into classes and objects. This improves code organization and promotes code reuse.

## 2. Naming Conventions

- **Consistent Naming:** Use clear and consistent naming conventions for variables, functions, classes, and UI elements. This improves code readability and makes it easier to understand the purpose of different code elements.
- **Meaningful Names:** Choose names that accurately reflect the purpose or functionality of the code element.

## 3. Code Style and Formatting

- **Consistent Style:** Follow a consistent coding style throughout your project. This improves code readability and makes it easier to collaborate with other developers.
- **Indentation and Spacing:** Use proper indentation and spacing to make your code more visually appealing and easier to follow.
- **Comments:** Add comments to explain complex logic, clarify assumptions, and document your code.

## 4. Design Patterns

- **Model-View-Controller (MVC) or Model-View-ViewModel (MVVM):** These patterns help separate the UI from the application logic, promoting maintainability and testability.
- **Observer Pattern:** Use the observer pattern to notify different parts of your application about changes in data or state.
- **Other Patterns:** Explore other design patterns that are relevant to your application's needs, such as the Singleton pattern, Factory pattern, or Strategy pattern.

## 5. Code Reusability

- **Custom Widgets:** Create custom widgets to encapsulate reusable UI elements and their associated logic.
- **Helper Functions:** Extract common code into helper functions to avoid code duplication.
- **Libraries:** Consider creating libraries to package reusable code that can be shared across multiple projects.

## 6. Performance Considerations

- **Profiling:** Regularly profile your code to identify performance bottlenecks and optimize critical sections.

- **Efficient Algorithms and Data Structures:** Choose algorithms and data structures that are appropriate for the scale of your application.
- **Asynchronous Operations:** Use threads or asynchronous operations to avoid blocking the UI thread and maintain responsiveness.

### 7. Documentation

- **Code Comments:** Add clear and concise comments to explain your code.
- **API Documentation:** Generate API documentation (e.g., using Doxygen) to document your classes, functions, and interfaces.
- **User Manuals:** Create user manuals or tutorials to help users understand how to use your application.

### Example: Using MVC in a Qt Application

C++

```cpp
// Model (DataModel.h)

class DataModel : public QObject {

    // ... data and logic ...

};
```

```cpp
// View (MainWindow.h)

class MainWindow : public QMainWindow {

    // ... UI elements and event handling ...

};
```

```cpp
// Controller (MainController.h)

class MainController : public QObject {

    // ... connects the model and view, handles user
interactions ...

};
```

This example demonstrates a basic MVC structure in a Qt application. The model holds the data and logic, the view displays the data, and the controller handles user interactions and updates the model and view accordingly.

By following these best practices and applying them consistently, you can write GUI code that is maintainable, scalable, and adaptable to future changes. This will not only make your development process more efficient but also ensure that your applications remain robust and performant as they grow in complexity.

# Best Practices: Code organization, commenting, design patterns

Writing clean, well-organized, and well-documented code is essential for maintainability and scalability in GUI applications. This section delves deeper into best practices for code organization, commenting, and leveraging design patterns to create robust and adaptable GUI applications.

## 1. Code Organization

- **Modularization:**
  - **Divide and Conquer:** Break down your application into smaller, manageable modules with well-defined responsibilities. This makes it easier to understand, debug, and modify individual parts of the code.
  - **Example:** Separate modules for UI, data handling, network communication, and business logic.
- **File Structure:**
  - **Logical Grouping:** Organize your source files into folders based on their functionality (e.g., ui, models, controllers, network).
  - **Header Files:** Use header files (.h or .hpp) to declare classes, functions, and

variables, and separate implementation into source files (.cpp).

- **Code Structure within Files:**
  - **Clear Sections:** Group related code together within a file (e.g., constructors, public methods, private methods, event handlers).
  - **Ordering:** Define a consistent order for elements within a class (e.g., public members first, then protected, then private).

## 2. Commenting

- **Purposeful Comments:**
  - **Explain Why, Not What:** Focus on explaining the "why" behind your code, not just what it does. The code itself should be clear enough to explain the "what."
  - **Clarify Assumptions:** Document any assumptions or constraints in your code.
  - **Document Complex Logic:** Provide comments for complex algorithms, data structures, or UI interactions.
- **Types of Comments:**
  - **Header Comments:** Add comments at the beginning of files to explain their purpose and contents.

- **Class and Function Comments:** Document classes and functions with their purpose, parameters, return values, and any exceptions they might throw.
- **Inline Comments:** Use inline comments sparingly to explain specific lines or blocks of code.
- **Commenting Styles:**
  - **Single-line Comments (//):** For brief comments or explanations.
  - **Multi-line Comments (/* */):** For longer explanations or documentation blocks.
  - **Doc Comments (/// or /** */):** For generating documentation with tools like Doxygen.

## 3. Design Patterns

Design patterns provide reusable solutions to common software design problems. They can help you create more maintainable, scalable, and flexible GUI applications.

- **Model-View-Controller (MVC):**
  - **Separation of Concerns:** Separates data (Model), presentation (View), and logic (Controller).
  - **Benefits:** Improves code organization, testability, and maintainability.

- **Model-View-ViewModel (MVVM):**
    - **Data Binding:** Connects the View and ViewModel through data binding, allowing automatic updates.
    - **Benefits:** Simplifies UI development and promotes code reusability.
- **Observer Pattern:**
    - **Notifications:** Allows objects (observers) to be notified of changes in another object (subject).
    - **Benefits:** Decouples objects and promotes modularity.
- **Singleton Pattern:**
    - **Single Instance:** Ensures that a class has only one instance and provides a global point of access.
    - **Benefits:** Useful for managing shared resources or application-wide settings.
- **Factory Pattern:**
    - **Object Creation:** Provides an interface for creating objects without specifying the exact class.
    - **Benefits:** Promotes flexibility and code reuse.

**Example: Commenting a Function**

C++

```
/**

 * @brief Calculates the factorial of a number.

 *

 * This function calculates the factorial of a non-negative
integer.

 *

 * @param n The input number.

 * @return The factorial of n.

 * @throw std::invalid_argument if n is negative.

 */

int factorial(int n) {

    // ... implementation ...

}
```

By applying these best practices for code organization, commenting, and utilizing design patterns, you can create GUI applications that are not only functional but also easy to understand, maintain, and scale over time.

This will improve your development efficiency and ensure that your applications remain robust and adaptable as they evolve.

# Chapter 14: Beyond the Basics

## Integrating with Third-Party Libraries

Modern GUI applications often leverage third-party libraries to add functionality, enhance visuals, or streamline development.[1] These libraries can provide anything from advanced charting capabilities to specialized image processing tools. This section explores the process of integrating third-party libraries into your C++ GUI applications, whether you're using wxWidgets or Qt.

### 1. Why Use Third-Party Libraries?

- **Save Time and Effort:** Avoid reinventing the wheel by using pre-built solutions for common tasks.[2]
- **Access Specialized Functionality:** Gain access to features not readily available in wxWidgets or Qt (e.g., advanced charting, image processing, scientific computing).
- **Improve User Experience:** Enhance your application with features like rich text editing, multimedia support, or 3D graphics.
- **Focus on Core Logic:** Concentrate on your application's core logic by delegating specific tasks to specialized libraries.[3]

## 2. Choosing the Right Library

- **Functionality:** Does the library provide the features you need?
- **License:** Is the library's license compatible with your project (e.g., open-source, commercial)?
- **Documentation:** Is the library well-documented with clear examples and tutorials?
- **Community Support:** Is there an active community or support forum for the library?
- **Maintenance:** Is the library actively maintained and updated?
- **Platform Compatibility:** Does the library support your target platforms (Windows, macOS, Linux)?

## 3. Integration Process

- **Obtain the Library:** Download the library's source code or pre-built binaries.
- **Build the Library (if necessary):** If you have the source code, you might need to build the library for your target platform and compiler.
- **Link the Library:** Configure your project's build settings to link against the library (static or dynamic linking).
- **Include Headers:** Include the library's header files in your code to access its functionality.

- **Follow the Library's API:** Use the library's API documentation and examples to integrate its features into your application.

### 4. wxWidgets Integration

- **Build Systems:** wxWidgets often uses build systems like CMake or autotools. You might need to integrate the third-party library into your wxWidgets project's build system.
- **Event Handling:** If the library generates events, you might need to integrate its event handling mechanism with wxWidgets' event system.

### 5. Qt Integration

- **Qt Creator:** Qt Creator provides mechanisms for adding external libraries to your project.[4]
- **Signals and Slots:** If the library uses signals and slots, you can connect them to your Qt signals and slots for seamless integration.

### 6. Example: Integrating a Charting Library (Qt with QCustomPlot)

- **Obtain QCustomPlot:** Download the QCustomPlot source code.
- **Add to Project:** Add the QCustomPlot source files to your Qt project.[5]
- **Include Headers:** Include the qcustomplot.h header file in your code.

- **Use QCustomPlot:** Create a QCustomPlot widget and use its API to add graphs, set data, and customize the chart's appearance.

C++

```
#include <qcustomplot.h>

// ... in your widget's constructor ...
QCustomPlot *customPlot = new QCustomPlot(this);
// ... add the customPlot widget to your layout ...


// ... later, when you want to plot data ...
customPlot->addGraph();
customPlot->graph(0)->setData(xData, yData);
customPlot->xAxis->setLabel("X Axis");
customPlot->yAxis->setLabel("Y Axis");
customPlot->replot();
```

## 7. Best Practices

- **Abstraction:** Create wrapper classes or functions to abstract the library's API and make it easier to use and maintain within your application.[6]
- **Error Handling:** Implement robust error handling to gracefully handle any errors or exceptions that the library might throw.
- **Dependency Management:** Use a dependency management system (e.g., Conan, vcpkg) to simplify the process of obtaining and managing third-party libraries.[7]
- **Keep Libraries Updated:** Regularly update your third-party libraries to benefit from bug fixes, performance improvements, and new features.

Integrating third-party libraries can significantly enhance the functionality and user experience of your C++ GUI applications. By carefully selecting libraries, following best practices, and understanding the integration process, you can leverage the power of external libraries to create more sophisticated and feature-rich applications.

## Exploring Emerging GUI Technologies

The landscape of GUI technology is constantly evolving, with new approaches and paradigms emerging to enhance user experiences and push the boundaries of human-computer interaction. This section explores some of the most promising emerging GUI technologies that are shaping the future of interface design.

## 1. Augmented Reality (AR) and Virtual Reality (VR)

AR and VR technologies are transforming how we interact with digital content by overlaying digital information onto the real world (AR) or immersing users in entirely virtual environments (VR).

- **AR in GUIs:**
  - **Contextual Information:** Overlaying information, instructions, or interactive elements onto real-world objects.
  - **Enhanced Visualization:** Visualizing data or 3D models in the context of the real world.
  - **Interactive Experiences:** Creating interactive AR experiences that blend the physical and digital worlds.
- **VR in GUIs:**
  - **Immersive Environments:** Designing UIs for virtual environments, allowing users to interact with 3D spaces and objects.
  - **Spatial Computing:** Creating interfaces that respond to user movements and gestures in 3D space.

- Data Visualization: Visualizing complex data in immersive 3D environments for better understanding and analysis.

## 2. Artificial Intelligence (AI)

AI is revolutionizing many aspects of computing, and GUI design is no exception.

- **Personalized Experiences:** AI can be used to personalize user interfaces based on user preferences, behavior, and context.
- **Intelligent Assistance:** AI-powered assistants can guide users through complex tasks, provide helpful suggestions, and automate repetitive actions.
- **Adaptive Interfaces:** UIs can adapt to different devices, screen sizes, and user needs using AI.
- **Natural Language Interaction:** AI enables more natural and intuitive interaction with GUIs through voice commands and natural language processing.

## 3. Voice User Interfaces (VUIs)

VUIs are becoming increasingly prevalent with the rise of voice assistants and smart speakers.

- **Voice Control:** Controlling applications and devices through voice commands.

- **Conversational Interfaces:** Designing interfaces that allow users to interact with applications through natural conversations.
- **Accessibility:** VUIs can improve accessibility for users with disabilities.

## 4. Gesture-Based Interfaces

Gesture recognition technology is enabling more intuitive and natural interaction with GUIs.

- **Touchless Control:** Controlling devices and applications with hand gestures or body movements.
- **Immersive Experiences:** Creating more immersive and engaging experiences in AR/VR environments.
- **Accessibility:** Gesture-based interfaces can provide alternative input methods for users with disabilities.

## 5. Brain-Computer Interfaces (BCIs)

BCIs are a cutting-edge technology that allows direct communication between the brain and a computer.

- **Future Potential:** While still in early stages, BCIs hold the potential to revolutionize GUI design by enabling users to control interfaces with their thoughts.

## 6. Haptic Feedback

Haptic feedback provides tactile sensations to the user, enhancing the sense of realism and immersion in GUIs.

- **Tactile Feedback:** Using vibrations or other haptic feedback mechanisms to provide confirmation of actions or simulate textures and physical interactions.

## 7. Flexible and Foldable Displays

Flexible and foldable displays are opening up new possibilities for GUI design.

- **Adaptive UIs:** Creating UIs that adapt to different screen shapes and sizes.
- **New Form Factors:** Exploring new device form factors and interaction paradigms.

## 8. Challenges and Considerations

- **Usability:** Ensure that new GUI technologies are intuitive and easy to use.
- **Accessibility:** Design interfaces that are accessible to users with disabilities.
- **Privacy and Security:** Address privacy and security concerns related to new technologies like AI and BCIs.
- **Technological Maturity:** Some emerging technologies are still in early stages of

development. Consider the maturity and feasibility of these technologies before integrating them into your applications.

By staying informed about these emerging GUI technologies and exploring their potential, you can prepare for the future of interface design and create innovative and user-centric applications.

## Continuous Learning and Community Resources

The world of C++ GUI development is dynamic and ever-evolving. To stay ahead of the curve and continue growing as a developer, it's essential to embrace continuous learning and tap into the wealth of knowledge and support available within the wxWidgets and Qt communities. This section highlights valuable resources and strategies for ongoing learning and community engagement.

### 1. Official Documentation

Both wxWidgets and Qt have extensive official documentation that serves as a primary source of information.

- **wxWidgets:**

- Online Documentation: https://docs.wxwidgets.org/
- **Reference Manual:** A comprehensive guide to wxWidgets classes and functions.
- **Tutorials:** Step-by-step guides for getting started with various wxWidgets topics.
- **Samples:** Example code demonstrating different wxWidgets features.

- **Qt:**

  - **Online Documentation:** https://doc.qt.io/
  - **Qt Assistant:** A searchable offline documentation tool.
  - **Qt Examples:** A vast collection of example code covering various Qt modules and functionalities.

## 2. Books and Tutorials

Numerous books and online tutorials cater to different learning styles and skill levels.

- **wxWidgets:**
  - **"Cross-Platform GUI Programming with wxWidgets" by Julian Smart and Kevin Hock**
  - **"wxWidgets Cookbook" by CodeLite**
  - **Online tutorials on websites like ZetCode and wxWiki.**
- **Qt:**

- "C++ GUI Programming with Qt 4" by Jasmin Blanchette and Mark Summerfield
- "Qt5 C++ GUI Programming Cookbook" by Lee Zhi Eng
- Online tutorials on the Qt website and other learning platforms.

## 3. Online Communities and Forums

Engage with the vibrant wxWidgets and Qt communities to seek help, share knowledge, and contribute to the open-source ecosystem.

- **wxWidgets:**
  - **Mailing Lists:** https://www.wxwidgets.org/support/mailing-lists/
  - **Forums:** https://forums.wxwidgets.org/
  - **IRC Channel:** #wxwidgets on Libera.Chat
- **Qt:**
  - **Qt Forum:** https://forum.qt.io/
  - **Mailing Lists:** https://lists.qt-project.org/
  - **IRC Channel:** #qt on Libera.Chat

## 4. Open-Source Projects

Explore the source code of open-source projects that use wxWidgets or Qt to learn from real-world examples and contribute to the community.

- **wxWidgets:** Audacity, Code::Blocks, FileZilla
- **Qt:** VLC media player, KDE desktop environment, Telegram

## 5. Continuous Learning Practices

- **Stay Updated:** Follow blogs, news sources, and social media to stay informed about the latest developments in wxWidgets, Qt, and GUI technologies in general.
- **Experiment:** Don't be afraid to experiment with new features, libraries, and techniques.
- **Contribute:** Contribute to the open-source community by reporting bugs, submitting patches, or writing documentation.
- **Share Your Knowledge:** Share your knowledge and experience with others through blog posts, tutorials, or presentations.

By actively engaging in continuous learning and participating in the wxWidgets and Qt communities, you can expand your skills, stay at the forefront of GUI development, and contribute to the advancement of these powerful frameworks.

# Links to online communities, forums, and documentation

Here's a curated list of links to valuable online resources for wxWidgets and Qt, including official documentation, community forums, mailing lists, and other helpful websites:

## wxWidgets

- **Official Website:** https://www.wxwidgets.org/
- **Documentation:** https://docs.wxwidgets.org/
- **Forums:** https://forums.wxwidgets.org/
- **Mailing Lists:** https://www.wxwidgets.org/support/mailing-lists/
- **Wiki:** https://wiki.wxwidgets.org/
- **wxPython (Python wrapper for wxWidgets):** https://www.wxpython.org/
- **wxPerl (Perl wrapper for wxWidgets):** https://metacpan.org/pod/Wx

## Qt

- **Official Website:** https://www.qt.io/
- **Documentation:** https://doc.qt.io/
- **Qt Forum:** https://forum.qt.io/
- **Mailing Lists:** https://lists.qt-project.org/
- **Wiki:** https://wiki.qt.io/
- **Qt Blog:** https://www.qt.io/blog

- **Qt Downloads:** https://www.qt.io/download
- **Qt for Python (PySide):** https://www.qt.io/qt-for-python

**Other Helpful Resources**

- **Stack Overflow:** A general programming Q&amp;A site with a large community and many questions related to wxWidgets and Qt.
- **GitHub:** Search for wxWidgets and Qt projects on GitHub to find open-source code examples and libraries.
- **Reddit:** Subreddits like r/wxWidgets and r/QtFramework can be good sources of information and discussion.

This list provides a starting point for exploring the wealth of online resources available for wxWidgets and Qt. Remember to bookmark these links and refer to them as you continue your journey in C++ GUI development.

# Appendices

# Appendix A: Common GUI Programming Errors and Solutions

GUI programming, while rewarding, can be prone to subtle errors that can lead to unexpected behavior, crashes, or visual glitches. This appendix provides a guide to common GUI programming errors, their potential causes, and effective solutions, helping you troubleshoot and debug your wxWidgets and Qt applications.

## 1. Layout Issues

- **Symptom:** Widgets overlapping, misaligned, or not visible.
- **Possible Causes:**
  - Incorrect sizer usage (wxWidgets) or layout manager settings (Qt).
  - Forgetting to set the sizer or layout on the parent widget.
  - Incorrect size policies or stretch factors.
  - Minimum size constraints not being respected.
  - Platform-specific differences in widget sizes or styles.
- **Solutions:**
  - Review sizer/layout settings and ensure proper nesting and proportions.

- Double-check that the sizer/layout is set on the parent widget.
- Adjust size policies and stretch factors to achieve the desired layout.
- Set minimum sizes for widgets to prevent them from being too small.
- Test on different platforms to identify and address platform-specific issues.

## 2. Event Handling Errors

- **Symptom:** Application not responding to user input, unexpected behavior when interacting with widgets.
- **Possible Causes:**
  - Incorrect event connections (signals and slots in Qt, event tables in wxWidgets).
  - Event handlers not being called or called in the wrong order.
  - Event propagation issues (events being blocked or not reaching the intended target).
- **Solutions:**
  - Verify signal/slot connections or event table entries.
  - Use debugging tools to trace event flow and ensure handlers are called correctly.
  - Review event filter logic and ensure events are propagated as expected.

○ Check for duplicate event handlers or conflicting connections.

## 3. Memory Management Problems

- **Symptom:** Application crashes, memory leaks, or performance degradation over time.
- **Possible Causes:**
  ○ Memory leaks due to forgetting to deallocate dynamically allocated memory.
  ○ Dangling pointers accessing invalid memory locations.
  ○ Accessing deleted objects or using uninitialized pointers.
- **Solutions:**
  ○ Use tools like Valgrind to detect memory leaks.
  ○ Employ RAII (Resource Acquisition Is Initialization) and smart pointers to manage memory automatically.
  ○ Be mindful of object ownership and ensure proper deallocation.
  ○ Initialize pointers before use and avoid accessing deleted objects.

## 4. Threading Issues

- **Symptom:** Application crashes, data corruption, or unpredictable behavior when using multiple threads.

- **Possible Causes:**
  - ○ Race conditions where multiple threads access shared data concurrently.
  - ○ Deadlocks where threads are blocked waiting for each other.
  - ○ Accessing GUI elements from non-GUI threads.
- **Solutions:**
  - ○ Use synchronization mechanisms (mutexes, semaphores) to protect shared data.
  - ○ Design your code to avoid deadlocks by acquiring locks in a consistent order.
  - ○ Use thread-safe methods (e.g., wxQueueEvent in wxWidgets, signals and slots with Qt::QueuedConnection in Qt) to communicate with the GUI thread.

## 5. Drawing and Rendering Errors

- **Symptom:** Visual glitches, artifacts, or incorrect rendering of graphics and text.
- **Possible Causes:**
  - ○ Incorrect use of drawing APIs (wxDC in wxWidgets, QPainter in Qt).
  - ○ Invalid coordinates, sizes, or transformations.
  - ○ Issues with image loading or manipulation.

- ○ Platform-specific rendering differences.
- **Solutions:**
  - ○ Review drawing code and ensure correct usage of drawing functions and parameters.
  - ○ Verify coordinates, sizes, and transformations for accuracy.
  - ○ Check for image format compatibility and proper loading procedures.
  - ○ Test on different platforms to identify and address rendering inconsistencies.

## 6. Resource Loading Problems

- **Symptom:** Missing images, icons, or other resources.
- **Possible Causes:**
  - ○ Incorrect resource paths or file names.
  - ○ Resource files not being included in the application bundle or installer.
  - ○ Platform-specific differences in resource loading mechanisms.
- **Solutions:**
  - ○ Verify resource paths and file names for accuracy.
  - ○ Ensure resource files are included in the application's distribution package.

- ○ Use platform-independent resource loading mechanisms provided by wxWidgets or Qt.

## 7. General Debugging Tips

- **Reproduce the Error:** Clearly identify the steps to reproduce the error consistently.
- **Isolate the Problem:** Narrow down the scope of the problem by systematically eliminating potential causes.
- **Use Debugging Tools:** Utilize debuggers, logging, and memory analysis tools to identify the root cause of the error.
- **Consult Documentation:** Refer to the official documentation and online resources for your chosen framework.
- **Seek Help from the Community:** Ask for help on forums or mailing lists if you encounter a particularly challenging problem.

By being aware of these common GUI programming errors and their solutions, you can effectively troubleshoot and debug your applications, ensuring they are robust, reliable, and provide a positive user experience.

# Appendix B: Useful Tools and Libraries

This appendix provides a curated list of useful tools and libraries that can enhance your C++ GUI development workflow, whether you're working with wxWidgets or Qt. These tools can assist with tasks ranging from UI design and debugging to image processing and data visualization.

## 1. UI Design Tools

- **Qt Designer (Qt):** A visual design tool integrated into Qt Creator for creating and editing Qt user interfaces.
- **Qt Design Studio (Qt):** A dedicated UI design tool for creating visually appealing and animated Qt Quick applications.
- **wxFormBuilder (wxWidgets):** A visual RAD tool for creating cross-platform wxWidgets user interfaces.
- **DialogBlocks (wxWidgets):** A commercial IDE with a visual dialog editor for wxWidgets.
- **Balsamiq Mockups:** A wireframing tool for quickly sketching UI layouts and prototypes.

## 2. Debugging and Profiling Tools

- **GDB (GNU Debugger):** A powerful command-line debugger for C++ applications.

- **Qt Creator Debugger (Qt):** A visual debugger integrated into Qt Creator.
- **Valgrind:** A memory debugging and profiling tool for detecting memory leaks and other memory-related errors.
- **gprof (GNU profiler):** A performance analysis tool for identifying code hotspots.

## 3. Build Systems

- **CMake:** A cross-platform build system generator that can be used with both wxWidgets and Qt.
- **qmake (Qt):** Qt's build system for managing Qt projects.
- **Autotools:** A collection of build tools often used with wxWidgets.

## 4. Image Processing Libraries

- **OpenCV:** A comprehensive open-source library for computer vision and image processing.
- **CImg:** A lightweight and header-only image processing library in C++.
- **Magick++:** The C++ API for ImageMagick, a powerful image manipulation library.

## 5. Data Visualization Libraries

- **QCustomPlot (Qt):** A Qt widget for creating 2D plots and charts.

- **Qwt (Qt):** A Qt widget library for technical applications, including plotting and data visualization.
- **wxFreeChart (wxWidgets):** A 2D charting library for wxWidgets.
- **wxMathPlot (wxWidgets):** A library for scientific plotting in wxWidgets.

## 6. Other Useful Libraries

- **Boost:** A collection of high-quality C++ libraries offering various functionalities (e.g., networking, multithreading, string manipulation).
- **Eigen:** A high-performance linear algebra library for C++.
- **SQLite:** A lightweight embedded database library often used in GUI applications for local data storage.

## 7. Tools for Cross-Platform Development

- **Virtual Machines:** Use virtual machines (e.g., VirtualBox, VMware) to test your application on different operating systems without needing separate physical machines.
- **Docker:** Containerization technology that can be used to create consistent development and testing environments across different platforms.

## 8. Version Control Systems

- **Git:** A popular distributed version control system for tracking code changes and collaborating with others.
- **Subversion (SVN):** A centralized version control system.

This list is not exhaustive, but it provides a good starting point for exploring tools and libraries that can enhance your C++ GUI development experience. Remember to research and choose the tools that best suit your project's specific needs and your preferred development workflow.

# Appendix C: C++ Quick Reference

This appendix provides a concise reference for essential C++ concepts and syntax, serving as a handy guide for developers working on GUI applications with wxWidgets or Qt.

## 1. Basic Syntax

- **Comments:**
    - Single-line: // This is a comment
    - Multi-line: /* This is a multi-line comment */
- **Data Types:**
    - int: Integer (whole numbers)
    - double: Double-precision floating-point number
    - char: Character
    - bool: Boolean (true or false)
    - string: String (sequence of characters)[1]
- **Variables:**
    - Declaration: int age;
    - Assignment: age = 25;
    - Initialization: int age = 25;
- **Operators:**
    - Arithmetic: +, -, *, /, % (modulo)
    - Comparison: ==, !=, >, <, >=, <=
    - Logical: && (and), || (or), ! (not)
    - Assignment: =, +=, -=, *=, /=, %=

- **Control Flow:**
  - if, else if, else: Conditional statements
  - for, while, do-while: Loops
  - switch: Switch statement

## 2. Functions

- **Definition:**

C++

```cpp
int add(int a, int b) {
    return a + b;
}
```

- **Calling:**

C++

```cpp
int sum = add(5, 3);
```

## 3. Object-Oriented Programming (OOP)

- **Classes:** Blueprints for creating objects.

C++

```cpp
class Dog {
public:
    string name;
    int age;

    void bark() {
        // ...
    }
};
```

- **Objects:** Instances of classes.

C++

```cpp
Dog myDog;
myDog.name = "Buddy";
```

- **Inheritance:** Creating new classes based on existing ones.

C++

```
class Poodle : public Dog {
    // ...
};
```

- **Polymorphism:** Using virtual functions to allow objects of different classes to be treated as objects of a common type.

## 4. Pointers

- **Declaration:** int *ptr;
- **Address-of operator:** ptr = &myVariable;
- **Dereference operator:** int value = *ptr;

## 5. Memory Management

- **Dynamic Allocation:** new, delete, new[], delete[]
- **RAII (Resource Acquisition Is Initialization):** Tie resource management to object lifetimes.
- **Smart Pointers:** std::unique_ptr, std::shared_ptr

## 6. Standard Template Library (STL)

- **Containers:** vector, list, map, set
- **Algorithms:** sort, find, for_each
- **Iterators:** Used to traverse containers

## 7. Input/Output (I/O)

- **iostream:** cout, cin, cerr
- **File I/O:** fstream, ifstream, ofstream

## 8. Error Handling

- **Exceptions:** try, catch, throw

## 9. Other

- **Namespaces:** using namespace std;
- **Preprocessor Directives:** #include, #define, #ifdef
- **Type Casting:** static_cast, dynamic_cast, reinterpret_cast

This quick reference provides a concise overview of essential C++ concepts. For more detailed information and advanced topics, refer to comprehensive C++ documentation and resources.